A Philosophy of Software Design

John Ousterhout
Stanford University

A Philosophy of Software Design
by John Ousterhout

Published by Yaknyam Press, Palo Alto, CA.

Cover design by Pete Nguyen and Shirin Oreizy (www.hellonextstep.com).

Printing History:
April 2018:   First Edition (v1.0)

ISBN 978-1-7321022-0-0

Contents

Contents

Preface

People have been writing programs for electronic computers for more than 80 years, but there has been surprisingly little conversation about how to design those programs or what good programs should look like. There has been considerable discussion about software development processes such as agile development and about development tools such as debuggers, version control systems, and test coverage tools. There has also been extensive analysis of programming techniques such as object-oriented programming and functional programming, and of design patterns and algorithms. All of these discussions have been valuable, but the core problem of software design is still largely untouched. David Parnas' classic paper "On the Criteria to be used in Decomposing Systems into Modules" appeared in 1971, but the state of the art in software design has not progressed much beyond that paper in the ensuing 45 years.

The most fundamental problem in computer science is *problem decomposition*: how to take a complex problem and divide it up into pieces that can be solved independently. Problem decomposition is the central design task that programmers face every day, and yet, other than the work described here, I have not been able to identify a single class in any university where problem decomposition is a central topic. We teach for loops and object-oriented programming, but not software design.

In addition, it is widely accepted that the best programmers are more than an order of magnitude better than average programmers, but we have made little attempt to understand what makes the best programmers so much better or to teach those skills in our classes. I have talked with several people I consider to be great programmers, but most of them had difficulty articulating specific techniques that give them their advantage. Many people assume that software design skill is an innate talent that cannot be taught. However, there is quite a bit of scientific evidence that outstanding performance in many fields is related more to high-quality practice than innate ability (see, for example, *Talent is Overrated* by Geoff Colvin).

For many years these issues have perplexed and frustrated me. I have wondered whether software design can be taught, and I have hypothesized that design skill is what separates great programmers from average ones. I finally decided that the only way to answer these questions was to attempt to teach a course on software design. The result is CS 190 at Stanford University. In this class I put forth a set of principles of software design. Students then work through a series of projects to assimilate and practice the principles. The class is taught in a fashion similar to a traditional English writing class. In an English class, students use an iterative process where they write a draft, get feedback, and then rewrite to make improvements. In CS 190, students develop a substantial piece of software from scratch. We then go through extensive code reviews to identify design problems, and students revise their projects to fix the problems. This allows students to see how their code can be improved by applying design principles.

I have now taught the software design class three times, and this book is based on the design principles that emerged from the class. The principles are fairly high level and border on the philosophical ("Define errors out of existence"), so it is hard for students to understand the ideas in the abstract. Students learn best by writing code, making mistakes, and then seeing how their mistakes and the subsequent fixes relate to the principles.

At this point you may well be wondering: what makes me think I know all the answers about software design? To be honest, I don't. There were no classes on software design when I learned to program, and I never had a mentor to teach me design principles. At the time I learned to program, code reviews were virtually nonexistent. My ideas about software design come from personal experience writing and reading code. Over my career I have written about 250,000 lines of code in a variety of languages. I've worked on teams that created three operating systems from scratch, multiple file and storage systems, infrastructure tools such as debuggers, build systems, and GUI toolkits, a scripting language, and interactive editors for text, drawings, presentations, and integrated circuits. Along the way I've experienced firsthand the problems of large systems and experimented with various design techniques. In addition, I've read a considerable amount of code written by other people, which has exposed me to a variety of approaches, both good and bad.

Out of all of this experience, I've tried to extract common threads, both about mistakes to avoid and techniques to use. This book is a reflection of my experiences: every problem described here is one that I have experienced personally, and every suggested technique is one that I have used successfully in my own coding.

I don't expect this book to be the final word on software design; I'm sure there are valuable techniques that I've missed, and some of my suggestions may turn out to be bad ideas in the long run. However, I hope that the book will start a conversation about software design. Compare the ideas in this book with your own experiences and decide for yourself whether the approaches described here really do reduce software complexity. This book is an opinion piece, so some readers will disagree with some of my suggestions. If you do disagree, try to understand why. I'm interested in hearing about things that work for you, things that don't work, and any other ideas you may have about software design. I hope that the ensuing conversations will improve our collective understanding of software design. I will incorporate what I learn in future editions of this book.

The best way to communicate with me about the book is to send email to the following address:

software-design-book@googlegroups.com

I'm interested in hearing specific feedback about the book, such as bugs or suggestions for improvement, as well as general thoughts and experiences related to software design. I'm particularly interested in compelling examples that I can use in future editions of the book. The best examples illustrate an important design principle and are simple enough to explain in a paragraph or two. If you would like to see what other people are saying on the email address and participate in discussions, you can join the Google Group software-design-book.

If for some reason the software-design-book Google Group should disappear in the future, search on the Web for my home page; it will contain updated instructions for how to communicate about the book. Please don't send book-related email to my personal email address.

I recommend that you take the suggestions in this book with a grain of salt. The overall goal is to reduce complexity; this is more important than any particular principle or idea you read here. If you try an idea from this book and find that it doesn't actually reduce complexity, then don't feel obligated to keep using it (but, do let me know about your experience; I'd like to get feedback on what works and what doesn't).

Many people have offered criticisms or made suggestions that improved the quality of the book. The following people offered helpful comments on various drafts of the book: Jeff Dean, Sanjay Ghemawat, John Hartman, Brian Kernighan, Amy Ousterhout, Kay Ousterhout, Rob Pike, and Keith Schwartz. Christos Kozyrakis suggested the terms "deep" and "shallow" for classes and interfaces, replacing previous terms "thick" and "thin", which were somewhat ambiguous. I am indebted to the students in CS 190; the process of reading their code and discussing it with them has helped to crystallize my thoughts about design.

Chapter 1

Introduction
(It's All About Complexity)

Writing computer software is one of the purest creative activities in the history of the human race. Programmers aren't bound by practical limitations such as the laws of physics; we can create exciting virtual worlds with behaviors that could never exist in the real world. Programming doesn't require great physical skill or coordination, like ballet or basketball. All programming requires is a creative mind and the ability to organize your thoughts. If you can visualize a system, you can probably implement it in a computer program.

This means that the greatest limitation in writing software is our ability to understand the systems we are creating. As a program evolves and acquires more features, it becomes complicated, with subtle dependencies between its components. Over time, complexity accumulates, and it becomes harder and harder for programmers to keep all of the relevant factors in their minds as they modify the system. This slows down development and leads to bugs, which slow development even more and add to its cost. Complexity increases inevitably over the life of any program. The larger the program, and the more people that work on it, the more difficult it is to manage complexity.

Good development tools can help us deal with complexity, and many great tools have been created over the last several decades. But there is a limit to what we can do with tools alone. If we want to make it easier to write software, so that we can build more powerful systems more cheaply, we must find ways to make software simpler. Complexity will still increase over time, in spite of our best efforts, but simpler designs allow us to build larger and more powerful systems before complexity becomes overwhelming.

There are two general approaches to fighting complexity, both of which will be

1

discussed in this book. The first approach is to eliminate complexity by making code simpler and more obvious. For example, complexity can be reduced by eliminating special cases or using identifiers in a consistent fashion.

The second approach to complexity is to encapsulate it, so that programmers can work on a system without being exposed to all of its complexity at once. This approach is called *modular design*. In modular design, a software system is divided up into *modules*, such as classes in an object-oriented language. The modules are designed to be relatively independent of each other, so that a programmer can work on one module without having to understand the details of other modules.

Because software is so malleable, software design is a continuous process that spans the entire lifecycle of a software system; this makes software design different from the design of physical systems such as buildings, ships, or bridges. However, software design has not always been viewed this way. For much of the history of programming, developers treated software design as something done once, at the beginning of a project. Development teams used what came to be called the *waterfall model*, in which a project is divided into discrete phases such as requirements definition, design, coding, testing, and maintenance. In the waterfall model, each phase completes before the next phase starts; in many cases different people are responsible for each phase. The entire system is designed at once, during the design phase. The design is frozen at the end of this phase, and the role of the subsequent phases is to flesh out and implement that design.

Unfortunately, the waterfall model rarely works well for software. Software systems are intrinsically more complex than physical systems; it isn't possible to visualize the design for a large software system well enough to understand all of its implications before building anything. As a result, the initial design will have many problems. The problems do not become apparent until implementation is well underway. However, the waterfall model is not structured to accommodate major design changes at this point (for example, the designers may have moved on to other projects). Thus, developers try to patch around the problems without changing the overall design. This results in an explosion of complexity.

Because of these issues, the waterfall model has been largely abandoned. Most software development projects today use an incremental approach such as *agile development*, in which the initial design focuses on a small subset of the overall functionality. This subset is designed, implemented, and then evaluated. Problems with the original design are discovered and corrected, then a few more features are designed, implemented and evaluated. Each iteration exposes problems with the existing design, which are fixed before the next set of features is designed. By spreading out the design in this way, problems with the initial design can be fixed while the system is still small; later features benefit from experience gained during the implementation of earlier features, so they have fewer problems.

The incremental approach works for software because software is malleable enough to allow significant design changes partway through implementation. In contrast, major design changes are much more challenging for physical systems: for example, it would not be practical to change the number of towers supporting a bridge in the middle of construction.

Incremental development means that software design is never done. Design happens continuously over the life of a system: developers should always be thinking about design issues. Incremental development also means continuous redesign. The initial design for a system or component is almost never the best one; experience inevitably shows better ways to do things. As a software developer, you should always be on the lookout for opportunities to improve the design of the system you are working on, and you should plan on spending some fraction of your time on design improvements.

If software developers should always be thinking about design issues, and reducing complexity is the most important element of software design, then software developers should always be thinking about complexity. This book is about how to use complexity to guide the design of software throughout its lifetime.

This book has two overall goals. The first is to describe the nature of software complexity: what does "complexity" mean, why does it matter, and how can you recognize when a program has unnecessary complexity? The book's second, and more challenging, goal is to present techniques you can use during the software development process to minimize complexity. Unfortunately, there isn't a simple recipe that will guarantee great software designs. Instead, I will present a collection of higher-level concepts that border on the philosophical, such as "classes should be deep" or "define errors out of existence." These concepts may not immediately identify the best design, but you can use them to compare design alternatives and guide your exploration of the design space.

1.1   How to use this book

Many of the design principles described here are somewhat abstract, so they may be hard to appreciate without looking at actual code. It has been a challenge to find examples that are small enough to include in the book, yet large enough to illustrate problems with real systems (if you encounter good examples, please send them to me). Thus, this book may not be sufficient by itself for you to learn how to apply the principles.

The best way to use this book is in conjunction with code reviews. When you read other people's code, think about whether it conforms to the concepts discussed here and how that relates to the complexity of the code. It's easier to see design problems in someone else's code than your own. You can use the red flags described here to identify problems and suggest improvements. Reviewing code will also expose you to new design approaches and programming techniques.

One of the best ways to improve your design skills is to learn to recognize *red flags*: signs that a piece of code is probably more complicated than it needs to be. Over the course of this book I will point out red flags that suggest problems related to each major design issue; the most important ones are summarized at the back of the book. You can then use these when you are coding: when you see a red flag, stop and look for an alternate design that eliminates the problem. When you first try this approach, you may have to try several design alternatives before you find one that eliminates the red flag. Don't give up easily: the more alternatives you try before fixing the problem, the more you will learn. Over time, you will find that your code has fewer and fewer red flags, and your designs are cleaner and cleaner. Your experience will also show you other red flags that you can use to identify design problems (I'd be happy to hear about these).

When applying the ideas from this book, it's important to use moderation and discretion. Every rule has its exceptions, and every principle has its limits. If you take any design idea to its extreme, you will probably end up in a bad place. Beautiful designs reflect a balance between competing ideas and approaches. Several chapters have sections titled "Taking it too far," which describe how to recognize when you are overdoing a good thing.

Almost all of the examples in this book are in Java or C++, and much of the discussion is in terms of designing classes in an object-oriented language. However, the ideas apply in other domains as well. Almost all of the ideas related to methods can also be applied to functions in a language without object-oriented features, such as C. The design ideas also apply to modules other than classes, such as subsystems or network services.

With this background, let's discuss in more detail what causes complexity, and how to make software systems simpler.

Chapter 2

The Nature of Complexity

This book is about how to design software systems to minimize their complexity. The first step is to understand the enemy. Exactly what is "complexity"? How can you tell if a system is unnecessarily complex? What causes systems to become complex? This chapter will address those questions at a high level; subsequent chapters will show you how to recognize complexity at a lower level, in terms of specific structural features.

The ability to recognize complexity is a crucial design skill. It allows you to identify problems before you invest a lot of effort in them, and it allows you to make good choices among alternatives. It is easier to tell whether a design is simple than it is to create a simple design, but once you can recognize that a system is too complicated, you can use that ability to guide your design philosophy towards simplicity. If a design appears complicated, try a different approach and see if that is simpler. Over time, you will notice that certain techniques tend to result in simpler designs, while others correlate with complexity. This will allow you to produce simpler designs more quickly.

This chapter also lays out some basic assumptions that provide a foundation for the rest of the book. Later chapters take the material of this chapter as given and use it to justify a variety of refinements and conclusions.

2.1   Complexity defined

For the purposes of this book, I define "complexity" in a practical way. **Complexity is anything related to the structure of a software system that makes it hard to understand and modify the system.** Complexity can take many forms. For example, it might be hard to understand how a piece of code works; it might take a lot of effort to implement a small improvement, or it might not be clear which parts of the system must be modified to make the improvement; it might be difficult to fix one bug without introducing another. If a software system is hard to understand and modify, then it is complicated; if it is easy to understand and modify, then it is simple.

You can also think of complexity in terms of cost and benefit. In a complex system, it takes a lot of work to implement even small improvements. In a simple system, larger improvements can be implemented with less effort.

Complexity is what a developer experiences at a particular point in time when trying to achieve a particular goal. It doesn't necessarily relate to the overall size or functionality of the system. People often use the word "complex" to describe large systems with sophisticated features, but if such a system is easy to work on, then, for the purposes of this book, it is not complex. Of course, almost all large and sophisticated software systems are in fact hard to work on, so they also meet my definition of complexity, but this need not necessarily be the case. It is also possible for a small and unsophisticated system to be quite complex.

Complexity is determined by the activities that are most common. If a system has a few parts that are very complicated, but those parts almost never need to be touched, then they don't have much impact on the overall complexity of the system. To characterize this in a crude mathematical way:

$$C = \sum_p c_p t_p$$

The overall complexity of a system (C) is determined by the complexity of each part p (c_p) weighted by the fraction of time developers spend working on that part (t_p). Isolating complexity in a place where it will never be seen is almost as good as eliminating the complexity entirely.

Complexity is more apparent to readers than writers. If you write a piece of code and it seems simple to you, but other people think it is complex, then it is complex. When you find yourself in situations like this, it's worth probing the other developers to find out why the code seems complex to them; there are probably some interesting lessons to learn from the disconnect between your opinion and theirs. Your job as a developer is not just to create code that you can work with easily, but to create code that others can also work with easily.

2.2 Symptoms of complexity

Complexity manifests itself in three general ways, which are described in the paragraphs below. Each of these manifestations makes it harder to carry out development tasks.

Change amplification: The first symptom of complexity is that a seemingly simple change requires code modifications in many different places. For example, consider a Web site containing several pages, each of which displays a banner with a background color. In many early Web sites, the color was specified explicitly on each page, as shown in Figure 2.1(a). In order to change the background for such a Web site, a developer might have to modify every existing page by hand; this would be nearly impossible for a large site with thousands of pages. Fortunately, modern Web sites use an approach like that in Figure 2.1(b), where the banner color is specified once in a central place, and all of the individual pages reference that shared value. With this approach, the banner color of the entire Web site can be changed with a single modification. One of the goals of good design is to reduce the amount of code that is affected by each design decision, so design changes don't require very many code modifications.

Cognitive load: The second symptom of complexity is cognitive load, which refers to how much a developer needs to know in order to complete a task. A higher cognitive load means that developers have to spend more time learning the required information, and there is a greater risk of bugs because they have missed something important. For example, suppose a function in C allocates memory, returns a pointer to that memory, and assumes that the caller will free the memory. This adds to the cognitive load of developers using the function; if a developer fails to free the memory, there will be a memory leak. If the system can be restructured so that the caller doesn't need to worry about freeing the memory (the same module that allocates the memory also takes responsibility for freeing it), it will reduce the cognitive load. Cognitive load arises in many ways, such as APIs with many methods, global variables, inconsistencies, and dependencies between modules.

System designers sometimes assume that complexity can be measured by lines of code. They assume that if one implementation is shorter than another, then it must be simpler; if it only takes a few lines of code to make a change, then the change must be easy. However, this view ignores the costs associated with cognitive load. I have seen frameworks that allowed applications to be written with only a few lines of code, but it was extremely difficult to figure out what those lines were. **Sometimes an approach**

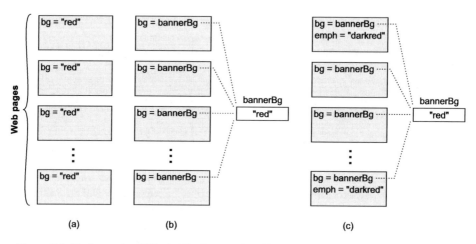

Figure 2.1: Each page in a Web site displays a colored banner. In (a) the background color for the banner is specified explicitly in each page. In (b) a shared variable holds the background color and each page references that variable. In (c) some pages display an additional color for emphasis, which is a darker shade of the banner background color; if the background color changes, the emphasis color must also change.

that requires more lines of code is actually simpler, because it reduces cognitive load.

Unknown unknowns: The third symptom of complexity is that it is not obvious which pieces of code must be modified to complete a task, or what information a developer must have to carry out the task successfully. Figure 2.1(c) illustrates this problem. The Web site uses a central variable to determine the banner background color, so it appears to be easy to change. However, a few Web pages use a darker shade of the background color for emphasis, and that darker color is specified explicitly in the individual pages. If the background color changes, then the the emphasis color must change to match. Unfortunately, developers are unlikely to realize this, so they may change the central `bannerBg` variable without updating the emphasis color. Even if a developer is aware of the problem, it won't be obvious which pages use the emphasis color, so the developer may have to search every page in the Web site.

Of the three manifestations of complexity, unknown unknowns are the worst. An unknown unknown means that there is something you need to know, but there is no way for you to find out what it is, or even whether there is an issue. You won't find out about it until bugs appear after you make a change. Change amplification is annoying, but as long as it is clear which code needs to be modified, the system will work once the change has been completed. Similarly, a high cognitive load will increase the cost of a change, but if it is clear which information to read, the change is still likely to be correct. With unknown unknowns, it is unclear what to do or whether a proposed solution will even work. The only way to be certain is to read every line of code in the system, which is impossible for systems of any size. Even this may not be sufficient, because a change may depend on a subtle design decision that was never documented.

One of the most important goals of good design is for a system to be *obvious*. This is the opposite of high cognitive load and unknown unknowns. In an obvious system, a developer can quickly understand how the existing code works and what is required to make a change. An obvious system is one where a developer can make a quick guess about what to do, without thinking very hard, and yet be confident that the guess is correct. Chapter 18 discusses techniques for making code more obvious.

2.3   Causes of complexity

Now that you know the high-level symptoms of complexity and why complexity makes software development difficult, the next step is to understand what causes complexity, so that we can design systems to avoid the problems. Complexity is caused by two things: *dependencies* and *obscurity*. This section discusses these factors at a high level; subsequent chapters will discuss how they relate to lower-level design decisions.

For the purposes of this book, a dependency exists when a given piece of code cannot be understood and modified in isolation; the code relates in some way to other code, and the other code must be considered and/or modified if the given code is changed. In the Web site example of Figure 2.1(a), the background color creates dependencies between all of the pages. All of the pages need to have the same background, so if the background is changed for one page, then it must be changed for all of them. Another example of dependencies occurs in network protocols. Typically there is separate code for the sender and receiver for the protocol, but they must each conform to the protocol; changing the code for the sender almost always requires corresponding changes at the receiver, and vice versa. The signature of a method creates a dependency between the implementation of that method and the code that invokes it: if a new parameter is added to a method, all of the invocations of that method must be modified to specify that parameter.

Dependencies are a fundamental part of software and can't be completely eliminated. In fact, we intentionally introduce dependencies as part of the software design process. Every time you write a new class you create dependencies around the API for that class. However, one of the goals of software design is to reduce the number of dependencies and to make the dependencies that remain as simple and obvious as possible.

Consider the Web site example. In the old Web site with the background specified separately on each page, all of the Web pages were dependent on each other. The new Web site fixed this problem by specifying the background color in a central place and providing an API that individual pages use to retrieve that color when they are rendered. The new Web site eliminated the dependency between the pages, but it created a new dependency around the API for retrieving the background color. Fortunately, the new dependency is more obvious: it is clear that each individual Web page depends on the bannerBg color, and a developer can easily find all the places where the variable is used by searching for its name. Furthermore, compilers help to manage API dependencies: if the name of the shared variable changes, compilation errors will occur in any code that still uses the old name. The new Web site replaced a nonobvious and difficult-to-manage dependency with a simpler and more obvious one.

The second cause of complexity is obscurity. Obscurity occurs when important information is not obvious. A simple example is a variable name that is so generic that it doesn't carry much useful information (e.g., time). Or, the documentation for a variable might not specify its units, so the only way to find out is to scan code for places where the variable is used. Obscurity is often associated with dependencies, where it is not obvious that a dependency exists. For example, if a new error status is added to a system, it may be necessary to add an entry to a table holding string messages for each status, but the existence of the message table might not be obvious to a programmer looking at the status declaration. Inconsistency is also a major contributor to obscurity: if the same variable name is used for two different purposes, it won't be obvious to developer which of these purposes a particular variable serves.

In many cases, obscurity comes about because of inadequate documentation; Chapter 13 deals with this topic. However, obscurity is also a design issue. If a system has a clean and obvious design, then it will need less documentation. The need for extensive documentation is often a red flag that the design isn't quite right. The best way to reduce obscurity is by simplifying the system design.

Together, dependencies and obscurity account for the three manifestations of complexity described in Section 2.2. Dependencies lead to change amplification and a high cognitive load. Obscurity creates unknown unknowns, and also contributes to cognitive load. If we can find design techniques that minimize dependencies and obscurity, then we can reduce the complexity of software.

2.4 Complexity is incremental

Complexity isn't caused by a single catastrophic error; it accumulates in lots of small chunks. A single dependency or obscurity, by itself, is unlikely to affect significantly the maintainability of a software system. Complexity comes about because hundreds or thousands of small dependencies and obscurities build up over time. Eventually, there are so many of these small issues that every possible change to the system is affected by several of them.

The incremental nature of complexity makes it hard to control. It's easy to convince yourself that a little bit of complexity introduced by your current change is no big deal. However, if every developer takes this approach for every change, complexity accumulates rapidly. Once complexity has accumulated, it is hard to eliminate, since fixing a single dependency or obscurity will not, by itself, make a big difference. In order to slow the growth of complexity, you must adopt a "zero tolerance" philosophy, as discussed in Chapter 3.

2.5 Conclusion

Complexity comes from an accumulation of dependencies and obscurities. As complexity increases, it leads to change amplification, a high cognitive load, and unknown unknowns. As a result, it takes more code modifications to implement each new feature. In addition, developers spend more time acquiring enough information to make the change safely and, in the worst case, they can't even find all the information they need. The bottom line is that complexity makes it difficult and risky to modify an existing code base.

Chapter 3

Working Code Isn't Enough
(Strategic vs. Tactical Programming)

One of the most important elements of good software design is the mindset you adopt when you approach a programming task. Many organizations encourage a tactical mindset, focused on getting features working as quickly as possible. However, if you want a good design, you must take a more strategic approach where you invest time to produce clean designs and fix problems. This chapter discusses why the strategic approach produces better designs and is actually cheaper than the tactical approach over the long run.

3.1 Tactical programming

Most programmers approach software development with a mindset I call *tactical programming*. In the tactical approach, your main focus is to get something working, such as a new feature or a bug fix. At first glance this seems totally reasonable: what could be more important than writing code that works? However, tactical programming makes it nearly impossible to produce a good system design.

The problem with tactical programming is that it is short-sighted. If you're programming tactically, you're trying to finish a task as quickly as possible. Perhaps you have a hard deadline. As a result, planning for the future isn't a priority. You don't spend much time looking for the best design; you just want to get something working soon. You tell yourself that it's OK to add a bit of complexity or introduce a small kludge or two, if that allows the current task to be completed more quickly.

This is how systems become complicated. As discussed in the previous chapter,

complexity is incremental. It's not one particular thing that makes a system complicated, but the accumulation of dozens or hundreds of small things. If you program
tactically, each programming task will contribute a few of these complexities. Each
of them probably seems like a reasonable compromise in order to finish the current
task quickly. However, the complexities accumulate rapidly, especially if everyone is
programming tactically.

Before long, some of the complexities will start causing problems, and you will
begin to wish you hadn't taken those early shortcuts. But, you will tell yourself that
it's more important to get the next feature working than to go back and refactor existing code. Refactoring may help out in the long run, but it will definitely slow down
the current task. So, you look for quick patches to work around any problems you encounter. This just creates more complexity, which then requires more patches. Pretty
soon the code is a mess, but by this point things are so bad that it would take months
of work to clean it up. There's no way your schedule can tolerate that kind of delay,
and fixing one or two of the problems doesn't seem like it will make much difference,
so you just keep programming tactically.

If you have worked on a large software project for very long, I suspect you have
seen tactical programming at work and have experienced the problems that result.
Once you start down the tactical path, it's difficult to change.

Almost every software development organization has at least one developer who
takes tactical programming to the extreme: a *tactical tornado*. The tactical tornado
is a prolific programmer who pumps out code far faster than others but works in a
totally tactical fashion. When it comes to implementing a quick feature, nobody gets it
done faster than the tactical tornado. In some organizations, management treats tactical
tornadoes as heroes. However, tactical tornadoes leave behind a wake of destruction.
They are rarely considered heroes by the engineers who must work with their code
in the future. Typically, other engineers must clean up the messes left behind by the
tactical tornado, which makes it appear that those engineers (who are the real heroes)
are making slower progress than the tactical tornado.

3.2 Strategic programming

The first step towards becoming a good software designer is to realize that **working
code isn't enough.** It's not acceptable to introduce unnecessary complexities in order
to finish your current task faster. The most important thing is the long-term structure
of the system. Most of the code in any system is written by extending the existing code

base, so your most important job as a developer is to facilitate those future extensions. Thus, you should not think of "working code" as your primary goal, though of course your code must work. Your primary goal must be to produce a great design, which also happens to work. This is *strategic programming*.

Strategic programming requires an investment mindset. Rather than taking the fastest path to finish your current project, you must invest time to improve the design of the system. These investments will slow you down a bit in the short term, but they will speed you up in the long term. Some of the investments will be proactive. For example, it's worth taking a little extra time to find a simple design for each new class; rather than implementing the first idea that comes to mind, try a couple of alternative designs and pick the cleanest one. Try to imagine a few ways in which the system might need to be changed in the future and make sure that will be easy with your design. Writing good documentation is another example of a proactive investment.

Other investments will be reactive. No matter how much you invest up front, there will inevitably be mistakes in your design decisions. Over time, these mistakes will become obvious. When you discover a design problem, don't just ignore it or patch around it; take a little extra time to fix it. If you program strategically, you will continually make small improvements to the system design. This is the opposite of tactical programming, where you are continually adding small bits of complexity that cause problems in the future.

3.3 How much to invest?

So, what is the right amount of investment? A huge up-front investment, such as trying to design the entire system, won't be effective. This is the waterfall method, and we know it doesn't work. The ideal design tends to emerge in bits and pieces, as you get experience with the system. Thus, the best approach is to make lots of small investments on a continual basis, adding up to about 10–20% of your total development time. Your initial projects will thus take 10–20% longer than they would in a purely tactical approach. That extra time will result in a better software design, and you will start experiencing the benefits within a few months. It won't be long before you're developing at least 10–20% faster than you would if you had programmed tactically. At this point your investments become free: the benefits from your past investments will save enough time to cover the cost of future investments. You will quickly recover the cost of the initial investment. Figure 3.1 illustrates this phenomenon.

Conversely, if you program tactically, you will finish your first projects 10–20%

15

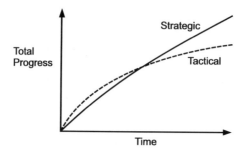

Figure 3.1: At the beginning, a tactical approach to programming will make progress more quickly than a strategic approach. However, complexity accumulates more rapidly under the tactical approach, which reduces productivity. Over time, the strategic approach results in greater progress.

faster, but over time your development speed will slow as complexity accumulates. It won't be long before you're programming at least 10–20% slower. You will quickly give back all of the time you saved at the beginning, and for the rest of system's lifetime you'll be developing more slowly than if you had taken the strategic approach. If you haven't ever worked in a badly degraded code base, talk to someone who has; they will tell you that poor code quality slows development by at least 20%.

3.4   Startups and investment

In some environments there are strong forces working against the strategic approach. For example, early-stage startups feel tremendous pressure to get their early releases out quickly. In these companies, it might seem that even a 10–20% investment isn't affordable. As a result, many startups take a tactical approach, spending little effort on design and even less on cleanup when problems pop up. They rationalize this with the thought that, if they are successful, they'll have enough money to hire extra engineers to clean things up.

If you are in a company leaning in this direction, you should realize that once a code base turns to spaghetti, it is nearly impossible to fix. You will probably pay high development costs for the life of the product. Furthermore, the payoff for good (or bad) design comes pretty quickly, so there's a good chance that the tactical approach won't even speed up your first product release.

Another thing to consider is that one of the most important factors for success of a company is the quality of its engineers. The best way to lower development costs is to hire great engineers: they don't cost much more than mediocre engineers but have tremendously higher productivity. However, the best engineers care deeply about good design. If your code base is a wreck, word will get out, and this will make it harder for you to recruit. As a result, you are likely to end up with mediocre engineers. This will increase your future costs and probably cause the system structure to degrade even more.

Facebook is an example of a startup that encouraged tactical programming. For many years the company's motto was "Move fast and break things." New engineers fresh out of college were encouraged to dive immediately into the company's code base; it was normal for engineers to push commits into production in their first week on the job. On the positive side, Facebook developed a reputation as a company that empowered its employees. Engineers had tremendous latitude, and there were few rules and restrictions to get in their way.

Facebook has been spectacularly successful as a company, but its code base became a mess: incomprehensible, unstable, few comments or tests, and painful to work with. Over time the company realized that its culture was unsustainable. Eventually, Facebook changed its motto to "Move fast with solid infrastructure" to encourage its engineers to invest more in good design. It remains to be seen whether Facebook can successfully clean up the problems that accumulated over years of tactical programming.

Fortunately, it is also possible to succeed in Silicon Valley with a strategic approach. Google and VMware grew up around the same time as Facebook, but both of these companies embraced a more strategic approach. Both companies placed a heavy emphasis on high quality code and good design, and both companies built sophisticated products that solved complex problems with reliable software systems. The companies' strong technical cultures became well known in Silicon Valley. Few other companies could compete with them for hiring the top technical talent.

These examples show that a company can succeed with either approach. However, it's a lot more fun to work in a company that cares about software design and has a clean code base.

17

3.5 Conclusion

Good design doesn't come for free. It has to be something you invest in continually, so that small problems don't accumulate into big ones. Fortunately, good design eventually pays for itself, and sooner than you might think.

It's crucial to be consistent in applying the strategic approach and to think of investment as something to do today, not tomorrow. When you get in a crunch it will be tempting to put off cleanups until after the crunch is over. However, this is a slippery slope; after the current crunch there will almost certainly be another one, and another after that. Once you start delaying design improvements, it's easy for the delays to become permanent and for your culture to slip into the tactical approach. The longer you wait to address design problems, the bigger they become; the solutions become more intimidating, which makes it easy to put them off even more. The most effective approach is one where every engineer makes continuous small investments in good design.

Chapter 4

Modules Should Be Deep

One of the most important techniques for managing software complexity is to design systems so that developers only need to face a small fraction of the overall complexity at any given time. This approach is called *modular design*, and this chapter presents its basic principles.

4.1 Modular design

In modular design, a software system is decomposed into a collection of *modules* that are relatively independent. Modules can take many forms, such as classes, subsystems, or services. In an ideal world, each module would be completely independent of the others: a developer could work in any of the modules without knowing anything about any of the other modules. In this world, the complexity of a system would be the complexity of its worst module.

Unfortunately, this ideal is not achievable. Modules must work together by calling each others's functions or methods. As a result, modules must know something about each other. There will be dependencies between the modules: if one module changes, other modules may need to change to match. For example, the arguments for a method create a dependency between the method and any code that invokes the method. If the required arguments change, all invocations of the method must be modified to conform to the new signature. Dependencies can take many other forms, and they can be quite subtle. The goal of modular design is to minimize the dependencies between modules.

In order to manage dependencies, we think of each module in two parts: an *interface* and an *implementation*. The interface consists of everything that a developer working in a different module must know in order to use the given module. Typically, the interface describes *what* the module does but not *how* it does it. The implementation consists of the code that carries out the promises made by the interface. A developer working in a particular module must understand the interface and implementation of that module, plus the interfaces of any other modules invoked by the given module. A developer should not need to understand the implementations of modules other than the one he or she is working in.

Consider a module that implements balanced trees. The module probably contains sophisticated code for ensuring that the tree remains balanced. However, this complexity is not visible to users of the module. Users see a relatively simple interface for invoking operations to insert, remove, and fetch nodes in the tree. To invoke an insert operation, the caller need only provide the key and value for the new node; the mechanisms for traversing the tree and splitting nodes are not visible in the interface.

For the purposes of this book, a module is any unit of code that has an interface and an implementation. Each class in an object-oriented programming language is a module. Methods within a class, or functions in a language that isn't object-oriented, can also be thought of as modules: each of these has an interface and an implementation, and modular design techniques can be applied to them. Higher-level subsystems and services are also modules; their interfaces may take different forms, such as kernel calls or HTTP requests. Much of the discussion about modular design in this book focuses on designing classes, but the techniques and concepts apply to other kinds of modules as well.

The best modules are those whose interfaces are much simpler than their implementations. Such modules have two advantages. First, a simple interface minimizes the complexity that a module imposes on the rest of the system. Second, if a module is modified in a way that does not change its interface, then no other module will be affected by the modification. If a module's interface is much simpler than its implementation, there will be many aspects of the module that can be changed without affecting other modules.

4.2   What's in an interface?

The interface to a module contains two kinds of information: formal and informal. The formal parts of an interface are specified explicitly in the code, and some of these can checked for correctness by the programming language. For example, the formal interface for a method is its signature, which includes the names and types of its parameters, the type of its return value, and information about exceptions thrown by the method.

Most programming languages ensure that each invocation of a method provides the right number and types of arguments to match its signature. The formal interface for a class consists of the signatures for all of its public methods, plus the names and types of any public variables.

Each interface also includes informal elements. These are not specified in a way that can be understood or enforced by the programming language. The informal parts of an interface include its high-level behavior, such as the fact that a function deletes the file named by one of its arguments. If there are constraints on the usage of a class (perhaps one method must be called before another), these are also part of the class's interface. In general, if a developer needs to know a particular piece of information in order to use a module, then that information is part of the module's interface. The informal aspects of an interface can only be described using comments, and the programming language cannot ensure that the description is complete or accurate. For most interfaces the informal aspects are larger and more complex than the formal aspects.

One of the benefits of a clearly specified interface is that it indicates exactly what developers need to know in order to use the associated module. This helps to eliminate the "unknown unknowns" problem described in Section 2.2.

4.3 Abstractions

The term *abstraction* is closely related to the idea of modular design. **An abstraction is a simplified view of an entity, which omits unimportant details.** Abstractions are useful because they make it easier for us to think about and manipulate complex things.

In modular programming, each module provides an abstraction in form of its interface. The interface presents a simplified view of the module's functionality; the details of the implementation are unimportant from the standpoint of the module's abstraction, so they are omitted from the interface.

In the definition of abstraction, the word "unimportant" is crucial. The more unimportant details that are omitted from an abstraction, the better. However, a detail can only be omitted from an abstraction if it is unimportant. An abstraction can go wrong in two ways. First, it can include details that are not really important; when this happens, it makes the abstraction more complicated than necessary, which increases the cognitive load on developers using the abstraction. The second error is when an abstraction omits details that really are important. This results in obscurity: developers

21

looking only at the abstraction will not have all the information they need to use the abstraction correctly. An abstraction that omits important details is a *false abstraction*: it might appear simple, but in reality it isn't. The key to designing abstractions is to understand what is important, and to look for designs that minimize the amount of information that is important.

As an example, consider a file system. The abstraction provided by a file system omits many details, such as the mechanism for choosing which blocks on a storage device to use for the data in a given file. These details are unimportant to users of the file system (as long as the system provides adequate performance). However, some of the details of a file system's implementation are important to users. Most file systems cache data in main memory, and they may delay writing new data to the storage device in order to improve performance. Some applications, such as databases, need to know exactly when data is written through to storage, so they can ensure that data will be preserved after system crashes. Thus, the rules for flushing data to secondary storage must be visible in the file system's interface.

We depend on abstractions to manage complexity not just in programming, but pervasively in our everyday lives. A microwave oven contains complex electronics to convert alternating current into microwave radiation and distribute that radiation throughout the cooking cavity. Fortunately, users see a much simpler abstraction, consisting of a few buttons to control the timing and intensity of the microwaves. Cars provide a simple abstraction that allows us to drive them without understanding the mechanisms for electrical motors, battery power management, anti-lock brakes, cruise control, and so on.

4.4 Deep modules

The best modules are those that provide powerful functionality yet have simple interfaces. I use the term *deep* to describe such modules. To visualize the notion of depth, imagine that each module is represented by a rectangle, as shown in Figure 4.1. The area of each rectangle is proportional to the functionality implemented by the module. The top edge of a rectangle represents the module's interface; the length of that edge indicates the complexity of the interface. The best modules are deep: they have a lot of functionality hidden behind a simple interface. A deep module is a good abstraction because only a small fraction of its internal complexity is visible to its users.

Module depth is a way of thinking about cost versus benefit. The benefit provided by a module is its functionality. The cost of a module (in terms of system complex-

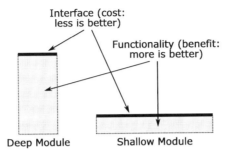

Figure 4.1: Deep and shallow modules. The best modules are deep: they allow a lot of functionality to be accessed through a simple interface. A shallow module is one with a relatively complex interface, but not much functionality: it doesn't hide much complexity.

ity) is its interface. A module's interface represents the complexity that the module imposes on the rest of the system: the smaller and simpler the interface, the less complexity that it introduces. The best modules are those with the greatest benefit and the least cost. Interfaces are good, but more, or larger, interfaces are not necessarily better!

The mechanism for file I/O provided by the Unix operating system and its descendants, such as Linux, is a beautiful example of a deep interface. There are only five basic system calls for I/O, with simple signatures:

```
int open(const char* path, int flags, mode_t permissions);
ssize_t read(int fd, void* buffer, size_t count);
ssize_t write(int fd, const void* buffer, size_t count);
off_t lseek(int fd, off_t offset, int referencePosition);
int close(int fd);
```

The open system call takes a hierarchical file name such as /a/b/c and returns an integer *file descriptor*, which is used to reference the open file. The other arguments for open provide optional information such as whether the file is being opened for reading or writing, whether a new file should be created if there is no existing file, and access permissions for the file, if a new file is created. The read and write system calls transfer information between buffer areas in the application's memory and the file; close ends the access to the file. Most files are accessed sequentially, so that is the default; however, random access can be achieved by invoking the lseek system call to change the current access position.

A modern implementation of the Unix I/O interface requires hundreds of thousands

23

of lines of code, which address complex issues such as:

- How are files represented on disk in order to allow efficient access?
- How are directories stored, and how are hierarchical path names processed to find the files they refer to?
- How are permissions enforced, so that one user cannot modify or delete another user's files?
- How are file accesses implemented? For example, how is functionality divided between interrupt handlers and background code, and how do these two elements communicate safely?
- What scheduling policies are used when there are concurrent accesses to multiple files?
- How can recently accessed file data be cached in memory in order to reduce the number of disk accesses?
- How can a variety of different secondary storage devices, such as disks and flash drives, be incorporated into a single file system?

All of these issues, and many more, are handled by the Unix file system implementation; they are invisible to programmers who invoke the system calls. Implementations of the Unix I/O interface have evolved radically over the years, but the five basic kernel calls have not changed.

Another example of a deep module is the garbage collector in a language such as Go or Java. This module has no interface at all; it works invisibly behind the scenes to reclaim unused memory. Adding garbage collection to a system actually shrinks its overall interface, since it eliminates the interface for freeing objects. The implementation of a garbage collector is quite complex, but that complexity is hidden from programmers using the language.

Deep modules such as Unix I/O and garbage collectors provide powerful abstractions because they are easy to use, yet they hide significant implementation complexity.

4.5 Shallow modules

On the other hand, a shallow module is one whose interface is relatively complex in comparison to the functionality that it provides. For example, a class that implements linked lists is shallow. It doesn't take much code to manipulate a linked list (inserting or deleting an element takes only a few lines), so the linked list abstraction doesn't hide very many details. The complexity of a linked list interface is nearly as great as the complexity of its implementation. Shallow classes are sometimes unavoidable, but they don't provide help much in managing complexity.

Here is an extreme example of a shallow method, taken from a project in a software design class:

```
private void addNullValueForAttribute(String attribute) {
    data.put(attribute, null);
}
```

From the standpoint of managing complexity, this method makes things worse, not better. The method offers no abstraction, since all of its functionality is visible through its interface. For example, callers probably need to know that the attribute will be stored in the `data` variable. It is no simpler to think about the interface than to think about the full implementation. If the method is documented properly, the documentation will be longer than the method's code. It even takes more keystrokes to invoke the method than it would take for a caller to manipulate the `data` variable directly. The method adds complexity (in the form of a new interface for developers to learn) but provides no compensating benefit.

4.6   Classitis

Unfortunately, the value of deep classes is not widely appreciated today. The conventional wisdom in programming is that classes should be *small*, not deep. Students are often taught that the most important thing in class design is to break up larger classes into smaller ones. The same advice is often given about methods: "Any method longer than N lines should be divided into multiple methods" (N can be as low as 10). This approach results in large numbers of shallow classes and methods, which add to overall

 Red Flag: Shallow Module

A shallow module is one whose interface is complicated relative to the functionality it provides. Shallow modules don't help much in the battle against complexity, because the benefit they provide (not having to learn about how they work internally) is negated by the cost of learning and using their interfaces. Small modules tend to be shallow.

system complexity.

The extreme of the "classes should be small" approach is a syndrome I call *classitis*, which stems from the mistaken view that "classes are good, so more classes are better." In systems suffering from classitis, developers are encouraged to minimize the amount of functionality in each new class: if you want more functionality, introduce more classes. Classitis may result in classes that are individually simple, but it produces tremendous complexity from the accumulated interfaces. It also tends to result in a verbose programming style from all of the boilerplate for each class.

4.7 Examples: Java and Unix I/O

One of the most visible examples of classitis today is the Java class library. The Java language doesn't require lots of small classes, but a culture of classitis seems to have taken root in the Java programming community. For example, to open a file in order to read serialized objects from it, you must create three different objects:

```
FileInputStream fileStream =
        new FileInputStream(fileName);
BufferedInputStream bufferedStream =
        new BufferedInputStream(fileStream);
ObjectInputStream objectStream =
        new ObjectInputStream(bufferedStream);
```

A FileInputStream object provides only rudimentary I/O: it is not capable of performing buffered I/O, nor can it read or write serialized objects. The BufferedInput-Stream object adds buffering to a FileInputStream, and the ObjectInputStream adds the ability to read and write serialized objects. The first two objects in the code above, fileStream and bufferedStream, are never used once the file has been opened; all future operations use objectStream.

It is particularly annoying (and error-prone) that buffering must be requested explicitly by creating a separate BufferedInputStream object; if a developer forgets to create this object, there will be no buffering and I/O will be slow. Perhaps the Java developers would argue that not everyone wants to use buffering for file I/O, so it shouldn't be built into the base mechanism. They might argue that it's better to keep buffering separate, so people can choose whether or not to use it. Providing choice is good, but **interfaces should be designed to make the common case as simple as possible** (see the formula on page 6). Almost every user of file I/O will want buffering, so it should be provided by default. For those few situations where buffering is not desirable, the library can provide a mechanism to disable it. Any mechanism

26

for disabling buffering should be cleanly separated in the interface (for example, by providing a different constructor for FileInputStream, or through a method that disables or replaces the buffering mechanism), so that most developers do not even need to be aware of its existence.

In contrast, the designers of the Unix system calls made the common case simple. For example, they recognized that sequential I/O is most common, so they made that the default behavior. Random access is still relatively easy to do, using the lseek system call, but a developer doing only sequential access need not be aware of that mechanism. If an interface has many features, but most developers only need to be aware of a few of them, the effective complexity of that interface is just the complexity of the commonly used features.

4.8 Conclusion

By separating the interface of a module from its implementation, we can hide the complexity of the implementation from the rest of the system. Users of a module need only understand the abstraction provided by its interface. The most important issue in designing classes and other modules is to make them deep, so that they have simple interfaces for the common use cases, yet still provide significant functionality. This maximizes the amount of complexity that is concealed.

Chapter 5

Information Hiding (and Leakage)

Chapter 4 argued that modules should be deep. This chapter, and the next few that follow, discuss techniques for creating deep modules.

5.1 Information hiding

The most important technique for achieving deep modules is *information hiding*. This technique was first described by David Parnas[1]. The basic idea is that each module should encapsulate a few pieces of knowledge, which represent design decisions. The knowledge is embedded in the module's implementation but does not appear in its interface, so it is not visible to other modules.

The information hidden within a module usually consists of details about how to implement some mechanism. Here are some examples of information that might be hidden within a module:

- How to store information in a B-tree, and how to access it efficiently.
- How to identify the physical disk block corresponding to each logical block within a file.
- How to implement the TCP network protocol.
- How to schedule threads on a multi-core processor.
- How to parse JSON documents.

The hidden information includes data structures and algorithms related to the mechanism. It can also include lower-level details such as the size of a page, and it can

---

[1] David Parnas, "On the Criteria to be Used in Decomposing Systems into Modules," *Communications of the ACM*, December 1972.

include higher-level concepts that are more abstract, such as an assumption that most files are small.

Information hiding reduces complexity in two ways. First, it simplifies the interface to a module. The interface reflects a simpler, more abstract view of the module's functionality and hides the details; this reduces the cognitive load on developers who use the module. For instance, a developer using a B-tree class need not worry about the ideal fanout for nodes in the tree or how to keep the tree balanced. Second, information hiding makes it easier to evolve the system. If a piece of information is hidden, there are no dependencies on that information outside the module containing the information, so a design change related to that information will affect only the one module. For example, if the TCP protocol changes (to introduce a new mechanism for congestion control, for instance), the protocol's implementation will have to be modified, but no changes should be needed in higher-level code that uses TCP to send and receive data.

When designing a new module, you should think carefully about what information can be hidden in that module. If you can hide more information, you should also be able to simplify the module's interface, and this makes the module deeper.

Note: hiding variables and methods in a class by declaring them `private` isn't the same thing as information hiding. Private elements can help with information hiding, since they make it impossible for the items to be accessed directly from outside the class. However, information about the private items can still be exposed through public methods such as getter and setter methods. When this happens the nature and usage of the variables are just as exposed as if the variables were public.

The best form of information hiding is when information is totally hidden within a module, so that it is irrelevant and invisible to users of the module. However, partial information hiding also has value. For example, if a particular feature or piece of information is only needed by a few of a class's users, and it is accessed through separate methods so that it isn't visible in the most common use cases, then that information is mostly hidden. Such information will create fewer dependencies than information that is visible to every user of the class.

5.2 Information leakage

The opposite of information hiding is *information leakage*. Information leakage occurs when a design decision is reflected in multiple modules. This creates a dependency between the modules: any change to that design decision will require changes to all of the involved modules. If a piece of information is reflected in the interface for a module, then by definition it has been leaked; thus, simpler interfaces tend to correlate with better information hiding. However, information can be leaked even if it doesn't appear in a module's interface. Suppose two classes both have knowledge of a particular file format (perhaps one class reads files in that format and the other class writes them). Even if neither class exposes that information in its interface, they both depend on the file format: if the format changes, both classes will need to be modified. Back-door leakage like this is more pernicious than leakage through an interface, because it isn't obvious.

Information leakage is one of the most important red flags in software design. One of the best skills you can learn as a software designer is a high level of sensitivity to information leakage. If you encounter information leakage between classes, ask yourself "How can I reorganize these classes so that this particular piece of knowledge only affects a single class?" If the affected classes are relatively small and closely tied to the leaked information, it may make sense to merge them into a single class. Another possible approach is to pull the information out of all of the affected classes and create a new class that encapsulates just that information. However, this approach will be effective only if you can find a simple interface that abstracts away from the details; if the new class exposes most of the knowledge through its interface, then it won't provide much value (you've simply replaced back-door leakage with leakage through an interface).

5.3   Temporal decomposition

One common cause of information leakage is a design style I call *temporal decomposition*. In temporal decomposition, the structure of a system corresponds to the time order in which operations will occur. Consider an application that reads a file in a par-

 Red Flag: Information Leakage

Information leakage occurs when the same knowledge is used in multiple places, such as two different classes that both understand the format of a particular type of file.

ticular format, modifies the contents of the file, and then writes the file out again. With temporal decomposition, this application might be broken into three classes: one to read the file, another to perform the modifications, and a third to write out the new version. Both the file reading and file writing steps have knowledge about the file format, which results in information leakage. The solution is to combine the core mechanisms for reading and writing files into a single class. This class will get used during both the reading and writing phases of the application. It's easy to fall into the trap of temporal decomposition, because the order in which operations must occur is often on your mind when you code. However, most design decisions manifest themselves at several different times over the life of the application; as a result, temporal decomposition often results in information leakage.

Order usually does matter, so it will be reflected somewhere in the application. However, it shouldn't be reflected in the module structure unless that structure is consistent with information hiding (perhaps the different stages use totally different information). **When designing modules, focus on the knowledge that's needed to perform each task, not the order in which tasks occur**.

5.4 Example: HTTP server

To illustrate the issues in information hiding, let's consider the design decisions made by students implementing the HTTP protocol in a software design course. It's useful to see both the things they did well and they areas where they had problems.

HTTP is a mechanism used by Web browsers to communicate with Web servers. When a user clicks on a link in a Web browser or submits a form, the browser uses HTTP to send a request over the network to a Web server. Once the server has pro-

 Red Flag: Temporal Decomposition

In temporal decomposition, execution order is reflected in the code structure: operations that happen at different times are in different methods or classes. If the same knowledge is used at different points in execution, it gets encoded in multiple places, resulting in information leakage.

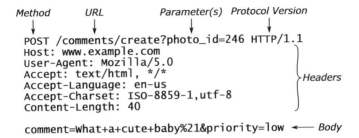

Figure 5.1: A POST request in the HTTP protocol consists of text sent over a TCP socket. Each request contains an initial line, a collection of headers terminated by an empty line, and an optional body. The initial line contains the request type (POST is used for submitting form data), a URL indicating an operation (/comments/create) and optional parameters (photo_id has the value 246), and the HTTP protocol version used by the sender. Each header line consists of a name such as Content-Length followed by its value. For this request, the body contains additional parameters (comment and priority).

cessed the request, it sends a response back to the browser; the response normally contains a new Web page to display. The HTTP protocol specifies the format of requests and responses, both of which are represented textually. Figure 5.1 shows a sample HTTP request describing a form submission. The students in the course were asked to implement one or more classes to make it easy for Web servers to receive incoming HTTP requests and send responses.

5.5 Example: too many classes

The most common mistake made by students was to divide their code into a large number of shallow classes, which led to information leakage between the classes. One team used two different classes for receiving HTTP requests; the first class read the request from the network connection into a string, and the second class parsed the string. This is an example of a temporal decomposition ("first we read the request, then we parse it"). Information leakage occurred because an HTTP request can't be read without parsing much of the message; for example, the Content-Length header specifies the length of the request body, so the headers must be parsed in order to compute the total request length. As a result, both classes needed to understand most of

33

the structure of HTTP requests, and parsing code was duplicated in both classes. This approach also created extra complexity for callers, who had to invoke two methods in different classes, in a particular order, to receive a request.

Because the classes shared so much information, it would have been better to merge them into a single class that handles both request reading and parsing. This provides better information hiding, since it isolates all knowledge of the request format in one class, and it also provides a simpler interface to callers (just one method to invoke).

This example illustrates a general theme in software design: **information hiding can often be improved by making a class slightly larger**. One reason for doing this is to bring together all of the code related to a particular capability (such as parsing an HTTP request), so that the resulting class contains everything related to that capability. A second reason for increasing the size of a class is to raise the level of the interface; for example, rather than having separate methods for each of three steps of a computation, have a single method that performs the entire computation. This can result in a simpler interface. Both of these benefits apply in the example of the previous paragraph: combining the classes brings together all of the code related to parsing an HTTP request, and it replaces two externally-visible methods with one. The combined class is deeper than the original classes.

Of course, it is possible to take the notion of larger classes too far (such as a single class for the entire application). Chapter 9 will discuss conditions under which it makes sense to separate code into multiple smaller classes.

5.6 Example: HTTP parameter handling

After an HTTP request has been received by a server, the server needs to access some of the information from the request. The code that handles the request in Figure 5.1 might need to know the value of the photo_id parameter. Parameters can be specified in the first line of the request (photo_id in Figure 5.1) or, sometimes, in the body (comment and priority in Figure 5.1). Each parameter has a name and a value. The values of parameters use a special encoding called *URL encoding*; for example, in the value for comment in Figure 5.1, "+" is used to represent a space character, and "%21" is used instead of "!". In order to process a request, the server will need the values for some of the parameters, and it will want them in unencoded form.

Most of the student projects made two good choices with respect to parameter handling. First, they recognized that server applications don't care whether a parameter

34

is specified in the header line or the body of the request, so they hid this distinction from callers and merged the parameters from both locations together. Second, they hid knowledge of URL encoding: the HTTP parser decodes parameter values before returning them to the Web server, so that the value of the comment parameter in Figure 5.1 will be returned as "What a cute baby!", not "What+a+cute+baby%21"). In both of these cases, information hiding resulted in simpler APIs for the code using the HTTP module.

However, most of the students used an interface for returning parameters that was too shallow, and this resulted in lost opportunities for information hiding. Most projects used an object of type HTTPRequest to hold the parsed HTTP request, and the HTTPRequest class had a single method like the following one to return parameters:

```
public Map<String, String> getParams() {
    return this.params;
}
```

Rather than returning a single parameter, the method returns a reference to the Map used internally to store all of the parameters. This method is shallow, and it exposes the internal representation used by the HTTPRequest class to store parameters. Any change to that representation will result in a change to the interface, which will require modifications to all callers. When implementations are modified, the changes often involve changes in the representation of key data structures (to improve performance, for example). Thus, it's important to avoid exposing internal data structures as much as possible. This approach also makes more work for callers: a caller must first invoke getParams, then it must call another method to retrieve a specific parameter from the Map. Finally, callers must realize that they should not modify the Map returned by getParams, since that will affect the internal state of the HTTPRequest.

Here is a better interface for retrieving parameter values:

```
public String getParameter(String name) { ... }
public int getIntParameter(String name) { ... }
```

getParameter returns a parameter value as a string. It provides a slightly deeper interface than getParams above; more importantly, it hides the internal representation of parameters. getIntParameter converts the value of a parameter from its string form in the HTTP request to an integer (e.g., the photo_id parameter in Figure 5.1). This saves the caller from having to request string-to-integer conversion separately, and hides that mechanism from the caller. Additional methods for other data types, such as getDoubleParameter, could be defined if needed. (All of these methods will throw exceptions if the desired parameter doesn't exist, or if it can't be converted to the requested type; the exception declarations have been omitted in the code above).

5.7   Example: defaults in HTTP responses

The HTTP projects also had to provide support for generating HTTP responses. The most common mistake students made in this area was inadequate defaults. Each HTTP response must specify an HTTP protocol version; one team required callers to specify this version explicitly when creating a response object. However, the response version must correspond to that in the request object, and the request must already be passed as an argument when sending the response (it indicates where to send the response). Thus, it makes more sense for the HTTP classes to provide the response version automatically. The caller is unlikely to know what version to specify, and if the caller does specify a value, it probably results in information leakage between the HTTP library and the caller. HTTP responses also include a Date header specifying the time when the response was sent; the HTTP library should provide a sensible default for this as well.

Defaults illustrate the principle that interfaces should be designed to make the common case as simple as possible. They are also an example of partial information hiding: in the normal case, the caller need not be aware of the existence of the defaulted item. In the rare cases where a caller needs to override a default, it will have to know about the value, and it can invoke a special method to modify it.

Whenever possible, classes should "do the right thing" without being explicitly asked. Defaults are an example of this. The Java I/O example on page 26 illustrates this point in a negative way. Buffering in file I/O is so universally desirable that no-one should ever have to ask explicitly for it, or even be aware of its existence; the I/O classes should do the right thing and provide it automatically. The best features are the

 Red Flag: Overexposure

If the API for a commonly used feature forces users to learn about other features that are rarely used, this increases the cognitive load on users who don't need the rarely used features.

ones you get without even knowing they exist.

5.8   Information hiding within a class

The examples in this chapter focused on information hiding as it relates to the externally visible APIs for classes, but information hiding can also be applied at other levels
in the system, such as within a class. Try to design the private methods within a class
so that each method encapsulates some information or capability and hides it from the
rest of the class. In addition, try to minimize the number of places where each instance
variable is used. Some variables may need to be accessed widely across the class, but
others may be needed in only a few places; if you can reduce the number of places
where a variable is used, you will eliminate dependencies within the class and reduce
its complexity.

5.9   Taking it too far

Information hiding only makes sense when the information being hidden is not needed
outside its module. If the information is needed outside the module, then you must *not*
hide it. Suppose that the performance of a module is affected by certain configuration
parameters, and that different uses of the module will require different settings of the
parameters. In this case it is important that the parameters are exposed in the interface
of the module, so that they can be turned appropriately. As a software designer, your
goal should be to minimize the amount of information needed outside a module; for
example, if a module can automatically adjust its configuration, that is better then
exposing configuration parameters. But, it's important to recognize which information
is needed outside a module and make sure it is exposed.

5.10   Conclusion

Information hiding and deep modules are closely related. If a module hides a lot of
information, that tends to increase the amount of functionality provided by the module
while also reducing its interface. This makes the module deeper. Conversely, if a
module doesn't hide much information, then either it doesn't have much functionality,
or it has a complex interface; either way, the module is shallow.

When decomposing a system into modules, try not to be influenced by the order in which operations will occur at runtime; that will lead you down the path of temporal decomposition, which will result in information leakage and shallow modules. Instead, think about the different pieces of knowledge that are needed to carry out the tasks of your application, and design each module to encapsulate one or a few of those pieces of knowledge. This will produce a clean and simple design with deep modules.

Chapter 6

General-Purpose Modules are Deeper

One of the most common decisions that you will face when designing a new module is whether to implement it in a general-purpose or special-purpose fashion. Some might argue that you should take a general-purpose approach, in which you implement a mechanism that can be used to address a broad range of problems, not just the ones that are important today. In this case, the new mechanism may find unanticipated uses in the future, thereby saving time. The general-purpose approach seems consistent with the investment mindset discussed in Chapter 3, where you spend a bit more time up front to save time later on.

On the other hand, we know that it's hard to predict the future needs of a software system, so a general-purpose solution might include facilities that are never actually needed. Furthermore, if you implement something that is too general-purpose, it might not do a good job of solving the particular problem you have today. As a result, some might argue that it's better to focus on today's needs, building just what you know you need, and specializing it for the way you plan to use it today. If you take the special-purpose approach and discover additional uses later, you can always refactor it to make it general-purpose. The special-purpose approach seems consistent with an incremental approach to software development.

6.1   Make classes somewhat general-purpose

In my experience, the sweet spot is to implement new modules in a *somewhat general-purpose* fashion. The phrase "somewhat general-purpose" means that the module's functionality should reflect your current needs, but its interface should not. Instead, the interface should be general enough to support multiple uses. The interface should be easy to use for today's needs without being tied specifically to them. The word "somewhat" is important: don't get carried away and build something so general-purpose that it is difficult to use for your current needs.

The most important (and perhaps surprising) benefit of the general-purpose approach is that it results in simpler and deeper interfaces than a special-purpose approach. The general-purpose approach can also save you time in the future, if you reuse the class for other purposes. However, even if the module is only used for its original purpose, the general-purpose approach is still better because of its simplicity.

6.2   Example: storing text for an editor

Let's consider an example from a software design class in which students were asked to build simple GUI text editors. The editors had to display a file and allow users to point, click, and type to edit the file. The editors had to support multiple simultaneous views of the same file in different windows; they also had to support multi-level undo and redo for modifications to the file.

Each of the student projects included a class that managed the underlying text of the file. The text classes typically provided methods for loading a file into memory, reading and modifying the text of the file, and writing the modified text back to a file.

Many of the student teams implemented special-purpose APIs for the text class. They knew that the class was going to be used in an interactive editor, so they thought about the features that the editor had to provide and tailored the API of the text class to those specific features. For example, if a user of the editor typed the backspace key, the editor deleted the character immediately to the left of the cursor; if the user typed the delete key, the editor deleted the character immediately to the right of the cursor. Knowing this, some of the teams created one method in the text class to support each of these specific features:

```
void backspace(Cursor cursor);
void delete(Cursor cursor);
```

Each of these methods takes the cursor position as its argument; a special type Cursor represents this position. The editor also had to support a selection that could be copied or deleted. The students handled this by defining a `Selection` class and passing an object of this class to the text class during deletions:

```
void deleteSelection(Selection selection);
```

The students probably thought that it would be easier to implement the user interface if the methods of the text class corresponded to the features visible to users. In reality, however, this specialization provided little benefit for the user interface code, and it created a high cognitive load for developers working on either the user interface or the text class. The text class ended up with a large number of shallow methods, each of which was only suitable for one user interface operation. Many of the methods, such as `delete`, were only invoked in a single place. As a result, a developer working on the user interface had to learn about a large number of methods for the text class.

This approach created information leakage between the user interface and the text class. Abstractions related to the user interface, such as the selection or the backspace key, were reflected in the text class; this increased the cognitive load for developers working on the text class. Each new user interface operation required a new method to be defined in the text class, so a developer working on the user interface was likely to end up working on the text class as well. One of the goals in class design is to allow each class to be developed independently, but the specialized approach tied the user interface and text classes together.

6.3   A more general-purpose API

A better approach is to make the text class more generic. Its API should be defined only in terms of basic text features, without reflecting the higher-level operations that will be implemented with it. For example, only two methods are needed for modifying text:

```
void insert(Position position, String newText);
void delete(Position start, Position end);
```

The first method inserts an arbitrary string at an arbitrary position within the text, and the second method deletes all of the characters at positions greater than or equal to `start` but less than `end`. This API also uses a more generic type `Position` instead of `Cursor`, which reflects a specific user interface. The text class should also provide general-purpose facilities for manipulating positions within the text, such as the following:

41

```
Position changePosition(Position position, int numChars);
```
This method returns a new position that is a given number of characters away from a given position. If the numChars argument is positive, the new position is later in the file than position; if numChars is negative, the new position is before position. The method automatically skips to the next or previous line when necessary. With these methods, the delete key can be implemented with the following code (assuming the cursor variable holds the current cursor position):
```
text.delete(cursor, text.changePosition(cursor, 1));
```
Similarly, the backspace key can be implemented as follows:
```
text.delete(text.changePosition(cursor, -1), cursor);
```
With the general-purpose text API, the code to implement user interface functions such as delete and backspace is a bit longer than with the original approach using a specialized text API. However, the new code is more obvious than the old code. A developer working in the user interface module probably cares about which characters are deleted by the backspace key. With the new code, this is obvious. With the old code, the developer had to go to the text class and read the documentation and/or code of the backspace method to verify the behavior. Furthermore, the general-purpose approach has less code overall than the specialized approach, since it replaces a large number of special-purpose methods in the text class with a smaller number of general-purpose ones.

A text class implemented with the general-purpose interface could potentially be used for other purposes besides an interactive editor. As one example, suppose you were building an application that modified a specified file by replacing all occurrences of a particular string with another string. Methods from the specialized text class, such as backspace and delete, would have little value for this application. However, the general-purpose text class would already have most of the functionality needed for the new application. All that is missing is a method to search for the next occurrence of a given string, such as this:
```
Position findNext(Position start, String string);
```
Of course, an interactive text editor is likely to have a mechanism for searching and replacing, in which case the text class would already include this method.

6.4 Generality leads to better information hiding

The general-purpose approach provides a cleaner separation between the text and user interface classes, which results in better information hiding. The text class need not be aware of specifics of the user interface, such as how the backspace key is handled; these details are now encapsulated in the user interface class. New user interface features can be added without creating new supporting functions in the text class. The general-purpose interface also reduces cognitive load: a developer working on the user interface only needs to learn a few simple methods, which can be reused for a variety of purposes.

The backspace method in the original version of the text class was a false abstraction. It purported to hide information about which characters are deleted, but the user interface module really needs to know this; user interface developers are likely to read the code of the backspace method in order to confirm its precise behavior. Putting the method in the text class just makes it harder for user interface developers to get the information they need. One of the most important elements of software design is determining who needs to know what, and when. When the details are important, it is better to make them explicit and as obvious as possible, such as the revised implementation of the backspace operation. Hiding this information behind an interface just creates obscurity.

6.5 Questions to ask yourself

It is easier to recognize a clean general-purpose class design than it is to create one. Here are some questions you can ask yourself, which will help you to find the right balance between general-purpose and special-purpose for an interface.

What is the simplest interface that will cover all my current needs? If you reduce the number of methods in an API without reducing its overall capabilities, then you are probably creating more general-purpose methods. The special-purpose text API had at least three methods for deleting text: backspace, delete, and deleteSelection. The more general-purpose API had only one method for deleting text, which served all three purposes. Reducing the number of methods makes sense only as long as the API for each individual method stays simple; if you have to introduce lots of additional arguments in order to reduce the number of methods, then you may not really be simplifying things.

In how many situations will this method be used? If a method is designed for one particular use, such as the backspace method, that is a red flag that it may be too special-purpose. See if you can replace several special-purpose methods with a single general-purpose method.

Is this API easy to use for my current needs? This question can help you to determine when you have gone too far in making an API simple and general-purpose. If you have to write a lot of additional code to use a class for your current purpose, that's a red flag that the interface doesn't provide the right functionality. For example, one approach for the text class would be to design it around single-character operations: insert inserts a single character and delete deletes a single character. This API is both simple and general-purpose. However, it would not be particularly easy to use for a text editor: higher-level code would contain lots of loops to insert or delete ranges of characters. The single-character approach would also be inefficient for large operations. Thus it's better for the text class to have built-in support for operations on ranges of characters.

6.6 Conclusion

General-purpose interfaces have many advantages over special-purpose ones. They tend to be simpler, with fewer methods that are deeper. They also provide a cleaner separation between classes, whereas special-purpose interfaces tend to leak information between classes. Making your modules somewhat general-purpose is one of the best ways to reduce overall system complexity.

Chapter 7

Different Layer, Different Abstraction

Software systems are composed in layers, where higher layers use the facilities provided by lower layers. In a well-designed system, each layer provides a different abstraction from the layers above and below it; if you follow a single operation as it moves up and down through layers by invoking methods, the abstractions change with each method call. For example:

- In a file system, the uppermost layer implements a file abstraction. A file consists of a variable-length array of bytes, which can be updated by reading and writing variable-length byte ranges. The next lower layer in the file system implements a cache in memory of fixed-size disk blocks; callers can assume that frequently used blocks will stay in memory where they can be accessed quickly. The lowest layer consists of device drivers, which move blocks between secondary storage devices and memory.
- In a network transport protocol such as TCP, the abstraction provided by the topmost layer is a stream of bytes delivered reliably from one machine to another. This level is built on a lower level that transmits packets of bounded size between machines on a best-effort basis: most packets will be delivered successfully, but some packets may be lost or delivered out of order.

If a system contains adjacent layers with similar abstractions, this is a red flag that suggests a problem with the class decomposition. This chapter discusses situations where this happens, the problems that result, and how to refactor to eliminate the problems.

7.1 Pass-through methods

When adjacent layers have similar abstractions, the problem often manifests itself in the form of *pass-through methods*. A pass-through method is one that does little except invoke another method, whose signature is similar or identical to that of the calling method. For example, a student project implementing a GUI text editor contained a class consisting almost entirely of pass-through methods. Here is an extract from that class:

```
public class TextDocument ... {
    private TextArea textArea;
    private WeakReference<TextDocumentListener> listener;
    ...
    public Character getLastTypedCharacter() {
        return textArea.getLastTypedCharacter();
    }
    public int getCursorOffset() {
        return textArea.getCursorOffset();
    }
    public void insertString(String textToInsert,
            int offset) {
        textArea.insertString(textToInsert, offset);
    }
    public void willInsertString(String stringToInsert,
            int offset) {
        if (listener != null && listener.get() != null) {
            listener.get().willInsertString(this,
                    stringToInsert, offset);
        }
    }
    ...
}
```

 Red Flag: Pass-Through Method

A pass-through method is one that does nothing except pass its arguments to another method, usually with the same API as the pass-through method. This typically indicates that there is not a clean division of responsibility between the classes.

13 of the 15 public methods in that class were pass-through methods.

Pass-through methods make classes shallower: they increase the interface complexity of the class, which adds complexity, but they don't increase the total functionality of the system. Of the four methods above, only the last one has any functionality, and even there it is trivial: the method checks the validity of one variable. Pass-through methods also create dependencies between classes: if the signature changes for the `insertString` method in `TextArea`, then the `insertString` method in `TextDocument` will have to change to match.

Pass-through methods indicate that there is confusion over the division of responsibility between classes. In the example above, the `TextDocument` class offers an `insertString` method, but the functionality for inserting text is implemented entirely in `TextArea`. This is usually a bad idea: the interface to a piece of functionality should be in the same class that implements the functionality. When you see pass-through methods from one class to another, consider the two classes and ask yourself "Exactly which features and abstractions is each of these classes responsible for?" You will probably notice that there is an overlap in responsibility between the classes.

The solution is to refactor the classes so that each class has a distinct and coherent set of responsibilities. Figure 7.1 illustrates several ways to do this. One approach, shown in Figure 7.1(b), is to expose the lower level class directly to the callers of the higher level class, removing all responsibility for the feature from the higher level class. Another approach is to redistribute the functionality between the classes, as in Figure 7.1(c). Finally, if the classes can't be disentangled, the best solution may be to merge them as in Figure 7.1(d).

In the example above, there were three classes with intertwined responsibilities: `TextDocument`, `TextArea`, and `TextDocumentListener`. The student eliminated the pass-through methods by moving methods between classes and collapsing the three classes into just two, whose responsibilities were more clearly differentiated.

7.2 When is interface duplication OK?

Having methods with the same signature is not always bad. The important thing is that each new method should contribute significant functionality. Pass-through methods are bad because they contribute no new functionality.

One example where it's useful for a method to call another method with the same signature is a *dispatcher*. A dispatcher is a method that uses its arguments to select one of several other methods to invoke; then it passes most or all of its arguments to

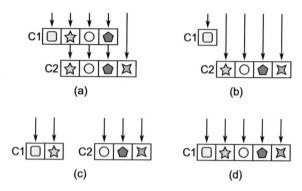

Figure 7.1: Pass-through methods. In (a), class C1 contains three pass-through methods, which do nothing but invoke methods with the same signature in C2 (each symbol represents a particular method signature). The pass-through methods can be eliminated by having C1's callers invoke C2 directly as in (b), by redistributing functionality between C1 and C2 to avoid calls between the classes as in (c), or by combining the classes as in (d).

the chosen method. The signature for the dispatcher is often the same as the signature for the methods that it calls. Even so, the dispatcher provides useful functionality: it chooses which of several other methods should carry out each task.

For example, when a Web server receives an incoming HTTP request from a Web browser, it invokes a dispatcher that examines the URL in the incoming request and selects a specific method to handle the request. Some URLs might be handled by returning the contents of a file on disk; others might be handled by invoking a procedure in a language such as PHP or JavaScript. The dispatch process can be quite intricate, and is usually driven by a set of rules that are matched against the incoming URL.

It is fine for several methods to have the same signature as long as each of them provides useful and distinct functionality. The methods invoked by a dispatcher have this property. Another example is interfaces with multiple implementations, such as disk drivers in an operating system. Each driver provides support for a different kind of disk, but they all have the same interface. When several methods provide different implementations of the same interface, it reduces cognitive load. Once you have worked with one of these methods, it's easier to work with the others, since you don't need to learn a new interface. Methods like this are usually in the same layer and they don't invoke each other.

7.3 Decorators

The decorator design pattern (also known as a "wrapper") is one that encourages API duplication across layers. A decorator object takes an existing object and extends its functionality; it provides an API similar or identical to the underlying object, and its methods invoke the methods of the underlying object. In the Java I/O example from Chapter 4, the BufferedInputStream class is a decorator: given an InputStream object, it provides the same API but introduces buffering. For example, when its read method is invoked to read a single character, it invokes read on the underlying InputStream to read a much larger block, and saves the extra characters to satisfy future read calls. Another example occurs in windowing systems: a Window class implements a simple form of window that is not scrollable, and a ScrollableWindow class decorates the Window class by adding horizontal and vertical scrollbars.

The motivation for decorators is to separate special-purpose extensions of a class from a more generic core. However, decorator classes tend to be shallow: they introduce a large amount of boilerplate for a small amount of new functionality. Decorator classes often contain many pass-through methods. It's easy to overuse the decorator pattern, creating a new class for every small new feature. This results in an explosion of shallow classes, such as the Java I/O example.

Before creating a decorator class, consider alternatives such as the following:

- Could you add the new functionality directly to the underlying class, rather than creating a decorator class? This makes sense if the new functionality is relatively general-purpose, or if it is logically related to the underlying class, or if most uses of the underlying class will also use the new functionality. For example, virtually everyone who creates a Java InputStream will also create a BufferedInputStream, and buffering is a natural part of I/O, so these classes should have been combined.

- If the new functionality is specialized for a particular use case, would it make sense to merge it with the use case, rather than creating a separate class?

- Could you merge the new functionality with an existing decorator, rather than creating a new decorator? This would result in a single deeper decorator class rather than multiple shallow ones.

- Finally, ask yourself whether the new functionality really needs to wrap the existing functionality: could you implement it as a stand-alone class that is independent of the base class? In the windowing example, the scrollbars could probably be implemented separately from the main window, without wrapping all of its existing functionality.

Sometimes decorators make sense, but there is usually a better alternative.

7.4 Interface versus implementation

Another application of the "different layer, different abstraction" rule is that the interface of a class should normally be different from its implementation: the representations used internally should be different from the abstractions that appear in the interface. If the two have similar abstractions, then the class probably isn't very deep. For example, in the text editor project discussed in Chapter 6, most of the teams implemented the text module in terms of lines of text, with each line stored separately. Some of the teams also designed the APIs for the text class around lines, with methods such as getLine and putLine. However, this made the text class shallow and awkward to use. In the higher-level user interface code, it's common to insert text in the middle of a line (e.g., when the user is typing) or to delete a range of text that spans lines. With a line-oriented API for the text class, callers were forced to split and join lines to implement the user-interface operations. This code was nontrivial and it was duplicated and scattered across the implementation of the user interface.

The text classes were much easier to use when they provided a character-oriented interface, such as an insert method that inserts an arbitrary string of text (which may include newlines) at an arbitrary position in the text and a delete method that deletes the text between two arbitrary positions in the text. Internally, the text was still represented in terms of lines. A character-oriented interface encapsulates the complexity of line splitting and joining inside the text class, which makes the text class deeper and simplifies higher level code that uses the class. With this approach, the text API is quite different from the line-oriented storage mechanism; the difference represents valuable functionality provided by the class.

7.5 Pass-through variables

Another form of API duplication across layers is a *pass-through variable*, which is a variable that is passed down through a long chain of methods. Figure 7.2(a) shows an example from a datacenter service. A command-line argument describes certificates to use for secure communication. This information is only needed by a low-level method m3, which calls a library method to open a socket, but it is passed down through all the methods on the path between main and m3. The cert variable appears in the signature of each of the intermediate methods.

Pass-through variables add complexity because they force all of the intermediate methods to be aware of their existence, even though the methods have no use for the variables. Furthermore, if a new variable comes into existence (for example, a system is initially built without support for certificates, but you later decide to add that support), you may have to modify a large number of interfaces and methods to pass the variable through all of the relevant paths.

Eliminating pass-through variables can be challenging. One approach is to see if there is already an object shared between the topmost and bottommost methods. In the datacenter service example of Figure 7.2, perhaps there is an object containing other information about network communication, which is available to both main and m3. If so, main can store the certificate information in that object, so it needn't be passed through all of the intervening methods on the path to m3 (see Figure 7.2(b)). However, if there is such an object, then it may itself be a pass-through variable (how else does m3 get access to it?).

Another approach is to store the information in a global variable, as in Figure 7.2(c). This avoids the need to pass the information from method to method, but global variables almost always create other problems. For example, global variables make it impossible to create two independent instances of the same system in the same process, since accesses to the global variables will conflict. It may seem unlikely that you would need multiple instances in production, but they are often useful in testing.

The solution I use most often is to introduce a *context* object as in Figure 7.2(d). A context stores all of the application's global state (anything that would otherwise be a pass-through variable or global variable). Most applications have multiple variables in their global state, representing things such as configuration options, shared subsystems, and performance counters. There is one context object per instance of the system. The context allows multiple instances of the system to coexist in a single process, each with its own context.

Unfortunately, the context will probably be needed in many places, so it can potentially become a pass-through variable. To reduce the number of methods that must be aware of it, a reference to the context can be saved in most of the system's major objects. In the example of Figure 7.2(d), the class containing m3 stores a reference to the context as an instance variable in its objects. When a new object is created, the

51

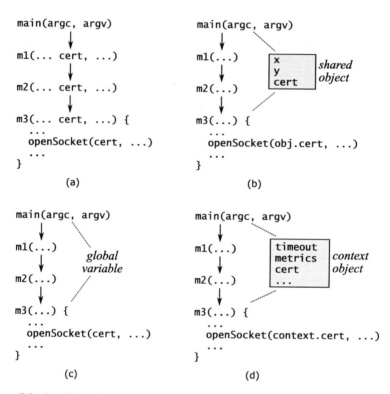

Figure 7.2: Possible techniques for dealing with a pass-through variable. In (a), cert is passed through methods m1 and m2 even though they don't use it. In (b), main and m3 have shared access to an object, so the variable can be stored there instead of passing it through m1 and m2. In (c), cert is stored as a global variable. In (d), cert is stored in a context object along with other system-wide information, such as a timeout value and performance counters; a reference to the context is stored in all objects whose methods need access to it.

creating method retrieves the context reference from its object and passes it to the constructor for the new object. With this approach, the context is available everywhere, but it only appears as an explicit argument in constructors.

The context object unifies the handling of all system-global information and eliminates the need for pass-through variables. If a new variable needs to be added, it can be added to the context object; no existing code is affected except for the constructor and destructor for the context. The context makes it easy to identify and manage the global state of the system, since it is all stored in one place. The context is also convenient for testing: test code can change the global configuration of the application by modifying fields in the context. It would be much more difficult to implement such changes if the system used pass-through variables.

Contexts are far from an ideal solution. The variables stored in a context have most of the disadvantages of global variables; for example, it may not be obvious why a particular variable is present, or where it is used. Without discipline, a context can turn into a huge grab-bag of data that creates nonobvious dependencies throughout the system. Contexts may also create thread-safety issues; the best way to avoid problems is for variables in a context to be immutable. Unfortunately, I haven't found a better solution than contexts.

7.6   Conclusion

Each piece of design infrastructure added to a system, such as an interface, argument, function, class, or definition, adds complexity, since developers must learn about this element. In order for an element to provide a net gain against complexity, it must eliminate some complexity that would be present in the absence of the design element. Otherwise, you are better off implementing the system without that particular element. For example, a class can reduce complexity by encapsulating functionality so that users of the class needn't be aware of it.

The "different layer, different abstraction" rule is just an application of this idea: if different layers have the same abstraction, such as pass-through methods or decorators, then there's a good chance that they haven't provided enough benefit to compensate for the additional infrastructure they represent. Similarly, pass-through arguments require each of several methods to be aware of their existence (which adds to complexity) without contributing additional functionality.

Chapter 8

Pull Complexity Downwards

This chapter introduces another way of thinking about how to create deeper classes. Suppose that you are developing a new module, and you discover a piece of unavoidable complexity. Which is better: should you let users of the module deal with the complexity, or should you handle the complexity internally within the module? If the complexity is related to the functionality provided by the module, then the second answer is usually the right one. Most modules have more users than developers, so it is better for the developers to suffer than the users. As a module developer, you should strive to make life as easy as possible for the users of your module, even if that means extra work for you. Another way of expressing this idea is that **it is more important for a module to have a simple interface than a simple implementation**.

As a developer, it's tempting to behave in the opposite fashion: solve the easy problems and punt the hard ones to someone else. If a condition arises that you're not certain how to deal with, the easiest thing is to throw an exception and let the caller handle it. If you are not certain what policy to implement, you can define a few configuration parameters to control the policy and leave it up to the system administrator to figure out the best values for them.

Approaches like these will make your life easier in the short term, but they amplify complexity, so that many people must deal with a problem, rather than just one person. For example, if a class throws an exception, every caller of the class will have to deal with it. If a class exports configuration parameters, every system administrator in every installation will have to learn how to set them.

8.1   Example: editor text class

Consider the class that manages the text of a file for a GUI text editor, which was discussed in Chapters 6 and 7. The class provides methods to read a file from disk into memory, query and modify the in-memory copy of the file, and write the modified version back to disk. When students had to implement this class, many of them chose a line-oriented interface, with methods to read, insert, and delete whole lines of text. This resulted in a simple implementation for the class, but it created complexity for higher level software. At the level of the user interface, operations rarely involve whole lines. For example, keystrokes cause individual characters to be inserted within an existing line; copying or deleting the selection can modify parts of several different lines. With the line-oriented text interface, higher-level software had to split and join lines in order to implement the user interface.

A character-oriented interface such as the one described in Section 6.3 pulls complexity downward. The user interface software can now insert and delete arbitrary ranges of text without splitting and merging lines, so it becomes simpler. The implementation of the text class probably becomes more complex: if it represents the text internally as a collection of lines, it will have to split and merge lines to implement the character-oriented operations. This approach is better because it encapsulates the complexity of splitting and merging within the text class, which reduces the overall complexity of the system.

8.2   Example: configuration parameters

Configuration parameters are an example of moving complexity upwards instead of down. Rather than determining a particular behavior internally, a class can export a few parameters that control its behavior, such as the size of a cache or the number of times to retry a request before giving up. Users of the class must then specify appropriate values for the parameters. Configuration parameters have become very popular in systems today; some systems have hundreds of them.

Advocates argue that configuration parameters are good because they allow users to tune the system for their particular requirements and workloads. In some situations it is hard for low-level infrastructure code to know the best policy to apply, whereas users are much more familiar with their domains. For instance, a user might know that some requests are more time-critical than others, so it makes sense for the user to specify a higher priority for those requests. In situations like this, configuration parameters can result in better performance across a broader variety of domains.

However, configuration parameters also provide an easy excuse to avoid dealing with important issues and pass them on to someone else. In many cases, it's difficult or impossible for users or administrators to determine the right values for the parameters. In other cases, the right values could have been determined automatically with a little extra work in the system implementation. Consider a network protocol that must deal with lost packets. If it sends a request but doesn't receive a response within a certain time period, it resends the request. One way to determine the retry interval is to introduce a configuration parameter. However, the transport protocol could compute a reasonable value on its own by measuring the response time for requests that succeed and then using a multiple of this for the retry interval. This approach pulls complexity downward and saves users from having to figure out the right retry interval. It has the additional advantage of computing the retry interval dynamically, so it will adjust automatically if operating conditions change. In contrast, configuration parameters can easily become out of date.

Thus, you should avoid configuration parameters as much as possible. Before exporting a configuration parameter, ask yourself: "will users (or higher-level modules) be able to determine a better value than we can determine here?" When you do create configuration parameters, see if you can compute reasonable defaults automatically, so users will only need to provide values under exceptional conditions. Ideally, each module should solve a problem completely; configuration parameters result in an incomplete solution, which adds to system complexity.

8.3 Taking it too far

Use discretion when pulling complexity downward; this is an idea that can easily be overdone. An extreme approach would be to pull all of the functionality of the entire application down into a single class, which clearly doesn't make sense. Pulling complexity down makes the most sense if (a) the complexity being pulled down is closely related to the class's existing functionality, (b) pulling the complexity down will result in many simplifications elsewhere in the application, and (c) pulling the complexity down simplifies the class's interface. Remember that the goal is to minimize overall system complexity.

Chapter 6 described how some students defined methods in the text class that reflected the user interface, such as a method that implements the functionality of the backspace key. It might seem that this is good, since it pulls complexity downward.

However, adding knowledge of the user interface to the text class doesn't simplify higher-level code very much, and the user-interface knowledge doesn't relate to the core functions of the text class. In this case, pulling complexity down just resulted in information leakage.

8.4 Conclusion

When developing a module, look for opportunities to take a little bit of extra suffering upon yourself in order to reduce the suffering of your users.

Chapter 9

Better Together Or Better Apart?

One of the most fundamental questions in software design is this: given two pieces of functionality, should they be implemented together in the same place, or should their implementations be separated? This question applies at all levels in a system, such as functions, methods, classes, and services. For example, should buffering be included in the class that provides stream-oriented file I/O, or should it be in a separate class? Should the parsing of an HTTP request be implemented entirely in one method, or should it be divided among multiple methods (or even multiple classes)? This chapter discusses the factors to consider when making these decisions. Some of these factors have already been discussed in previous chapters, but they will be revisited here for completeness.

When deciding whether to combine or separate, the goal is to reduce the complexity of the system as a whole and improve its modularity. It might appear that the best way to achieve this goal is to divide the system into a large number of small components: the smaller the components, the simpler each individual component is likely to be. However, the act of subdividing creates additional complexity that was not present before subdivision:

- Some complexity comes just from the number of components: the more components, the harder to keep track of them all and the harder to find a desired component within the large collection. Subdivision usually results in more interfaces, and every new interface adds complexity.
- Subdivision can result in additional code to manage the components. For example, a piece of code that used a single object before subdivision might now have to manage multiple objects.
- Subdivision creates separation: the subdivided components will be farther apart

than they were before subdivision. For example, methods that were together in a single class before subdivision may be in different classes after subdivision, and possibly in different files. Separation makes it harder for developers to see the components at the same time, or even to be aware of their existence. If the components are truly independent, then separation is good: it allows the developer to focus on a single component at a time, without being distracted by the other components. On the other hand, if there are dependencies between the components, then separation is bad: developers will end up flipping back and forth between the components. Even worse, they may not be aware of the dependencies, which can lead to bugs.

- Subdivision can result in duplication: code that was present in a single instance before subdivision may need to be present in each of the subdivided components.

Bringing pieces of code together is most beneficial if they are closely related. If the pieces are unrelated, they are probably better off apart. Here are a few indications that two pieces of code are related:

- They share information; for example, both pieces of code might depend on the syntax of a particular type of document.
- They are used together: anyone using one of the pieces of code is likely to use the other as well. This form of relationship is only compelling if it is bidirectional. As a counter-example, a disk block cache will almost always involve a hash table, but hash tables can be used in many situations that don't involve block caches; thus, these modules should be separate.
- They overlap conceptually, in that there is a simple higher-level category that includes both of the pieces of code. For example, searching for a substring and case conversion both fall under the category of string manipulation; flow control and reliable delivery both fall under the category of network communication.
- It is hard to understand one of the pieces of code without looking at the other.

The rest of this chapter uses more specific rules as well as examples to show when it makes sense to bring pieces of code together and when it makes sense to separate them.

9.1 Bring together if information is shared

Section 5.4 introduced this principle in the context of a project implementing an HTTP server. In its first implementation, the project used two different methods in different classes to read in and parse HTTP requests. The first method read the text of an incoming request from a network socket and placed it in a string object. The second method parsed the string to extract the various components of the request. With this decomposition, both of the methods ended up with considerable knowledge of the format of HTTP requests: the first method was only trying to read the request, not parse it, but it couldn't identify the end of the request without doing most of the work of parsing it (for example, it had to parse header lines in order to identify the header containing the overall request length). Because of this shared information, it is better to both read and parse the request in the same place; when the two classes were combined into one, the code got shorter and simpler.

9.2 Bring together if it will simplify the interface

When two or more modules are combined into a single module, it may be possible to define an interface for the new module that is simpler or easier to use than the original interfaces. This often happens when the original modules each implement part of the solution to a problem. In the HTTP server example from the preceding section, the original methods required an interface to return the HTTP request string from the first method and pass it to the second. When the methods were combined, these interfaces were eliminated.

In addition, when the functionality of two or more classes is combined, it may be possible to perform some functions automatically, so that most users need not be aware of them. The Java I/O library illustrates this opportunity. If the `FileInputStream` and `BufferedInputStream` classes were combined and buffering were provided by default, the vast majority of users would never even need to be aware of the existence of buffering. A combined `FileInputStream` class might provide methods to disable or replace the default buffering mechanism, but most users would not need to learn about them.

9.3 Bring together to eliminate duplication

If you find the same pattern of code repeated over and over, see if you can reorganize the code to eliminate the repetition. One approach is to factor the repeated code out into a separate method and replace the repeated code snippets with calls to the method. This approach is most effective if the repeated code snippet is long and the replacement method has a simple signature. If the snippet is only one or two lines long, there may not be much benefit in replacing it with a method call. If the snippet interacts in complex ways with its environment (such as by accessing numerous local variables), then the replacement method might require a complex signature (such as many pass-by-reference arguments), which would reduce its value.

Another way to eliminate duplication is to refactor the code so that the snippet in question only needs to be executed in one place. Suppose you are writing a method that needs to return errors at several different points, and the same cleanup actions need to be performed at each of these points before returning (see Figure 9.1 for an example). If the programming language supports goto, you can move the cleanup code to the very end of the method and then goto that snippet at each of the points where an error return is required, as in Figure 9.2. Goto statements are generally considered a bad idea, and they can result in indecipherable code if used indiscriminately, but they are useful in situations like this where they are used to escape from nested code.

9.4 Separate general-purpose and special-purpose code

If a module contains a mechanism that can be used for several different purposes, then it should provide just that one general-purpose mechanism. It should not include code that specializes the mechanism for a particular use, nor should it contain other general-purpose mechanisms. Special-purpose code associated with a general-purpose mechanism should normally go in a different module (typically one associated with the particular purpose). The GUI editor discussion in Chapter 6 illustrated this principle: the best design was one where the text class provided general-purpose text operations, while operations particular to the user interface (such as deleting the selection) were implemented in the user interface module. This approach eliminated information leakage and additional interfaces that were present in an earlier design where the specialized user interface operations were implemented in the text class.

 Red Flag: Repetition

If the same piece of code (or code that is almost the same) appears over and over again, that's a red flag that you haven't found the right abstractions.

```
switch (common->opcode) {
    case DATA: {
        DataHeader* header = received->getStart<DataHeader>();
        if (header == NULL) {
            LOG(WARNING, "%s packet from %s too short (%u bytes)",
                        opcodeSymbol(common->opcode),
                        received->sender->toString(),
                        received->len);
            return;
        }
        ...
    case GRANT: {
        GrantHeader* header = received->getStart<GrantHeader>();
        if (header == NULL) {
            LOG(WARNING, "%s packet from %s too short (%u bytes)",
                        opcodeSymbol(common->opcode),
                        received->sender->toString(),
                        received->len);
            return;
        }
        ...
    case RESEND: {
        ResendHeader* header = received->getStart<ResendHeader>();
        if (header == NULL) {
            LOG(WARNING, "%s packet from %s too short (%u bytes)",
                        opcodeSymbol(common->opcode),
                        received->sender->toString(),
                        received->len);
            return;
        }
        ...
}
```

Figure 9.1: This code processes incoming network packets of different types; for each type, if the packet is too short for that type, a message gets logged. In this version of the code, the LOG statement is duplicated for several different packet types.

```
switch (common->opcode) {
    case DATA: {
        DataHeader* header = received->getStart<DataHeader>();
        if (header == NULL)
            goto packetTooShort;
        ...
    case GRANT: {
        GrantHeader* header = received->getStart<GrantHeader>();
        if (header == NULL)
            goto packetTooShort;
        ...
    case RESEND: {
        ResendHeader* header = received->getStart<ResendHeader>();
        if (header == NULL)
            goto packetTooShort;
        ...
}
...
packetTooShort:
LOG(WARNING, "%s packet from %s too short (%u bytes)",
        opcodeSymbol(common->opcode),
        received->sender->toString(),
        received->len);
return;
```

Figure 9.2: A reorganization of the code from Figure 9.1 so that there is only one copy of the LOG statement.

In general, the lower layers of a system tend to be more general-purpose and the upper layers more special-purpose. For example, the topmost layer of an application consists of features totally specific to that application. The way to separate special-purpose code from general-purpose code is to pull the special-purpose code upwards, into the higher layers, leaving the lower layers general-purpose. When you encounter a class that includes both general-purpose and special-purpose features for the same abstraction, see if the class can be separated into two classes, one containing the general-purpose features, and the other layered on top of it to provide the special-purpose features.

64

9.5   Example: insertion cursor and selection

The next sections work through three examples that illustrate the principles discussed above. In two of the examples the best approach is to separate the relevant pieces of code; the third example it is better to join them together.

The first example consists of the insertion cursor and the selection in the GUI editor project from Chapter 6. The editor displayed a blinking vertical line indicating where text typed by the user would appear in the document. It also displayed a highlighted range of characters called the *selection*, which was used for copying or deleting text. The insertion cursor was always visible, but there could be times when no text was selected. If the selection existed, the insertion cursor was always positioned at one end of it.

The selection and insertion cursor are related in some ways. For example, the cursor is always positioned at one end of the selection, and the cursor and selection tend to be manipulated together: clicking and dragging the mouse sets both of them, and text insertion first deletes the selected text, if there is any, and then inserts new text at the cursor position. Thus, it might seem logical to use a single object to manage both the selection and the cursor, and one project team took this approach. The object stored two positions in the file, along with booleans indicating which end was the cursor and whether the selection existed.

However, the combined object was awkward. It provided no benefit for higher-level code, since the higher-level code still needed to be aware of the selection and cursor as distinct entities, and it manipulated them separately (during text insertion, it first invoked a method on the combined object to delete the selected text; then it invoked another method to retrieve the cursor position in order to insert new text).

 Red Flag: Special-General Mixture

This red flag occurs when a general-purpose mechanism also contains code specialized for a particular use of that mechanism. This makes the mechanism more complicated and creates information leakage between the mechanism and the particular use case: future modifications to the use case are likely to require changes to the underlying mechanism as well.

The combined object was actually more complex to implement than separate objects. It avoided storing the cursor position as a separate entity, but instead had to store a boolean indicating which end of the selection was the cursor. In order to retrieve the cursor position, the combined object had to first test the boolean and then choose the appropriate end of the selection.

In this case, the selection and cursor were not closely enough related to combine them. When the code was revised to separate the selection and the cursor, both the usage and the implementation became simpler. Separate objects provided a simpler interface than a combined object from which selection and cursor information had to be extracted. The cursor implementation also got simpler because the cursor position was represented directly, rather than indirectly through a selection and a boolean. In fact, in the revised version no special classes were used for either the selection or the cursor. Instead, a new `Position` class was introduced to represent a location in the file (a line number and character within line). The selection was represented with two `Positions` and the cursor with one. `Positions` also found other uses in the project. This example also demonstrates the benefits of a lower-level but more general-purpose interface, which were discussed in Chapter 6.

9.6   Example: separate class for logging

The second example involved error logging in a student project. A class contained several code sequences like the following:

```
try {
    rpcConn = connectionPool.getConnection(dest);
} catch (IOException e) {
    NetworkErrorLogger.logRpcOpenError(req, dest, e);
    return null;
}
```

Rather than logging the error at the point where it was detected, a separate method in a special error logging class was invoked. The error logging class was defined at the end of the same source file:

```
private static class NetworkErrorLogger {
    /**
     * Output information relevant to an error that occurs when trying
     * to open a connection to send an RPC.
     *
     * @param req
     *       The RPC request that would have been sent through
```

```
 *       the connection
 * @param dest
 *       The destination of the RPC
 * @param e
 *       The caught error
 */
public static void logRpcOpenError(RpcRequest req,
        AddrPortTuple dest, Exception e) {
    logger.log(Level.WARNING, "Cannot send message: " + req +
            ". \n" + "Unable to find or open connection to " +
            dest + " :" + e);
}
...
}
```

The NetworkErrorLogger class contained several methods such as logRpcSendError and logRpcReceiveError, each of which logged a different kind of error.

This separation added complexity with no benefit. The logging methods were shallow: most consisted of a single line of code, but they required a considerable amount of documentation. Each method was only invoked in a single place. The logging methods were highly dependent on their invocations: someone reading the invocation would most likely flip over to the logging method to make sure that the right information was being logged; similarly, someone reading the logging method would probably flip over to the invocation site to understand the purpose of the method.

In this example, it would be better to eliminate the logging methods and place the logging statements at the locations where the errors were detected. This would make the code easier to read and eliminate the interfaces required for the logging methods.

9.7   Example: editor undo mechanism

In the GUI editor project from Section 6.2, one of the requirements was to support multi-level undo/redo, not just for changes to the text itself, but also for changes in the selection, insertion cursor, and view. For example, if a user selected some text, deleted it, scrolled to a different place in the file, and then invoked undo, the editor had to restore its state to what it was just before the deletion. This included restoring the deleted text, selecting it again, and also making the selected text visible in the window.

Some of the student projects implemented the entire undo mechanism as part of the text class. The text class maintained a list of all the undoable changes. It automatically added entries to this list whenever the text was changed. For changes to the selection, insertion cursor, and view, the user interface code invoked additional methods in the text class, which then added entries for those changes to the undo list. When undo or redo was requested by the user, the user interface code invoked a method in the text class, which then processed the entries in the undo list. For entries related to text, it updated the internals of the text class; for entries related to other things, such as the selection, the text class called back to the user interface code to carry out the undo or redo.

This approach resulted in an awkward set of features in the text class. The core of undo/redo consists of a general-purpose mechanism for managing a list of actions that have been executed and stepping through them during undo and redo operations. The core was located in the text class along with special-purpose handlers that implemented undo and redo for specific things such as text and the selection. The special-purpose undo handlers for the selection and the cursor had nothing to do with anything else in the text class; they resulted in information leakage between the text class and the user interface, as well as extra methods in each module to pass undo information back and forth. If a new sort of undoable thing were added to the system in the future, it would require changes to the text class, including new methods specific to that undoable thing. In addition, the general-purpose undo core had little to do with the general-purpose text facilities in the class.

These problems can be solved by extracting the general-purpose core of the undo/redo mechanism and placing it in a separate class:

```
public class History {
    public interface Action {
        public void redo();
        public void undo();
    }

    History() {...}

    void addAction(Action action) {...}
    void addFence() {...}

    void undo() {...}
    void redo() {...}
}
```

In this design, the History class manages a collection of objects that implement the interface History.Action. Each History.Action describes a single operation, such as a text insertion or a change in the cursor location, and it provides methods that can undo or redo the operation. The History class knows nothing about the information stored in the actions or how they implement their undo and redo methods. History maintains a history list describing all of the actions executed over the lifetime of an application, and it provides undo and redo methods that walk backwards and forwards through the list in response to user-requested undos and redos, calling undo and redo methods in the History.Actions.

History.Actions are special-purpose objects: each one understands a particular kind of undoable operation. They are implemented outside the History class, in modules that understand a particular kinds of undoable action. The text class might implement UndoableInsert and UndoableDelete objects to describe text insertions and deletions. Whenever it inserts text, the text class creates a new UndoableInsert object describing the insertion and invokes History.addAction to add it to the history list. The editor's user interface code might create UndoableSelection and UndoableCursor objects that describe changes to the selection and insertion cursor.

The History class also allows actions to be grouped so that, for example, a single undo request from the user can restore deleted text, reselect the deleted text, and reposition the insertion cursor. There are a number of ways to group actions; the History class uses *fences*, which are markers placed in the history list to separate groups of related actions. Each call to History.redo walks backwards through the history list, undoing actions until it reaches the next fence. The placement of fences is determined by higher-level code by invoking History.addFence.

This approach divides the functionality of undo into three categories, each of which is implemented in a different place:

- A general-purpose mechanism for managing and grouping actions and invoking undo/redo operations (implemented by the History class).
- The specifics of particular actions (implemented by a variety of classes, each of which understands a small number of action types).
- The policy for grouping actions (implemented by high-level user interface code to provide the right overall application behavior).

Each of these categories can be implemented without any understanding of the other categories. The History class does not know what kind of actions are being undone; it could be used in a variety of applications. Each action class understands only a single kind of action, and neither the History class nor the action classes needs to be aware of the policy for grouping actions.

The key design decision was the one that separated the general-purpose part of the undo mechanism from the special-purpose parts and put the general-purpose part in a class by itself. Once that was done, the rest of the design fell out naturally.

Note: the suggestion to separate general-purpose code from special-purpose code refers to code related to a particular mechanism. For example, special-purpose undo code (such as code to undo a text insertion) should be separated from general-purpose undo code (such as code to manage the history list). However, it often makes sense to combine special-purpose code for one mechanism with general-purpose code for another. The text class is an example of this: it implements a general-purpose mechanism for managing text, but it includes special-purpose code related to undoing. The undo code is special-purpose because it only handles undo operations for text modifications. It doesn't make sense to combine this code with the general-purpose undo infrastructure in the History class, but it does make sense to put it in the text class, since it is closely related to other text functions.

9.8 Splitting and joining methods

The issue of when to subdivide applies not just to classes, but also to methods: are there times when it is better to divide an existing method into multiple smaller methods? Or, should two smaller methods be combined into one larger one? Long methods tend to be more difficult to understand than shorter ones, so many people argue that length alone is a good justification for breaking up a method. Students in classes are often given rigid criteria, such as "Split up any method longer than 20 lines!"

However, length by itself is rarely a good reason for splitting up a method. In general, developers tend to break up methods too much. Splitting up a method introduces additional interfaces, which add to complexity. It also separates the pieces of the original method, which makes the code harder to read if the pieces are actually related. You shouldn't break up a method unless it makes the overall system simpler; I'll discuss how this might happen below.

Long methods aren't always bad. For example, suppose a method contains five 20-line blocks of code that are executed in order. If the blocks are relatively independent, then the method can be read and understood one block at a time; there's not much benefit in moving each of the blocks into a separate method. If the blocks have complex interactions, it's even more important to keep them together so readers can see all of the code at once; if each block is in a separate method, readers will have to flip back and forth between these spread-out methods in order to understand how they work together. Methods containing hundreds of lines of code are fine if they have a simple signature and are easy to read. These methods are deep (lots of functionality, simple

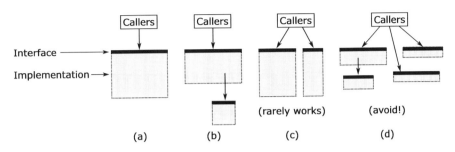

Figure 9.3: A method (a) can be split either by by extracting a subtask (b) or by dividing its functionality into two separate methods (c). A method should not be split if it results in shallow methods, as in (d).

interface), which is good.

When designing methods, the most important goal is to provide clean and simple abstractions. **Each method should do one thing and do it completely.** The method should have a clean and simple interface, so that users don't need to have much information in their heads in order to use it correctly. The method should be deep: its interface should be much simpler than its implementation. If a method has all of these properties, then it probably doesn't matter whether it is long or not.

Splitting up a method only makes sense if it results in cleaner abstractions, overall. There are two ways to do this, which are diagrammed in Figure 9.3. The best way is by factoring out a subtask into a separate method, as shown in Figure 9.3(b). The subdivision results in a child method containing the subtask and a parent method containing the remainder of the original method; the parent invokes the child. The interface of the new parent method is the same as the original method. This form of subdivision makes sense if there is a subtask that is cleanly separable from the rest of the original method, which means (a) someone reading the child method doesn't need to know anything about the parent method and (b) someone reading the parent method doesn't need to understand the implementation of the child method. Typically this means that the child method is relatively general-purpose: it could conceivably be used by other methods besides the parent. If you make a split of this form and then find yourself flipping back and forth between the parent and child to understand how they work together, that is a red flag ("Conjoined Methods") indicating that the split was probably a bad idea.

The second way to break up a method is to split it into two separate methods,

71

each visible to callers of the original method, as in Figure 9.3(c). This makes sense if the original method had an overly complex interface because it tried to do multiple things that were not closely related. If this is the case, it may be possible to divide the method's functionality into two or more smaller methods, each of which has only a part of the original method's functionality. If you make a split like this, the interface for each of the resulting methods should be simpler than the interface of the original method. Ideally, most callers should only need to invoke one of the two new methods; if callers must invoke both of the new methods, then that adds complexity, which makes it less likely that the split is a good idea. The new methods will be more focused in what they do. It is a good sign if the new methods are more general-purpose than the original method (i.e., you can imagine using them separately in other situations).

Splits of the form shown in Figure 9.3(c) don't make sense very often, because they result in callers having to deal with multiple methods instead of one. When you split this way, you run the risk of ending up with several shallow methods, as in Figure 9.3(d). If the caller has to invoke each of the separate methods, passing state back and forth between them, then splitting is not a good idea. If you're considering a split like the one in Figure 9.3(c), you should judge it based on whether it simplifies things for callers.

There are also situations where a system can be made simpler by joining methods together. For example, joining methods might replace two shallow methods with one deeper method; it might eliminate duplication of code; it might eliminate dependencies between the original methods, or intermediate data structures; it might result in better encapsulation, so that knowledge that was previously present in multiple places is now isolated in a single place; or it might result in a simpler interface, as discussed in Section 9.2.

Red Flag: Conjoined Methods

It should be possible to understand each method independently. If you can't understand the implementation of one method without also understanding the implementation of another, that's a red flag. This red flag can occur in other contexts as well: if two pieces of code are physically separated, but each can only be understood by looking at the other, that is a red flag.

9.9 Conclusion

The decision to split or join modules should be based on complexity. Pick the structure that results in the best information hiding, the fewest dependencies, and the deepest interfaces.

Chapter 10

Define Errors Out Of Existence

Exception handling is one of the worst sources of complexity in software systems. Code that deals with special conditions is inherently harder to write than code that deals with normal cases, and developers often define exceptions without considering how they will be handled. This chapter discusses why exceptions contribute disproportionately to complexity, then it shows how to simplify exception handling. The key overall lesson from this chapter is to reduce the number of places where exceptions must be handled; in many cases the semantics of operations can be modified so that the normal behavior handles all situations and there is no exceptional condition to report (hence the title of this chapter).

10.1 Why exceptions add complexity

I use the term *exception* to refer to any uncommon condition that alters the normal flow of control in a program. Many programming languages include a formal exception mechanism that allows exceptions to be thrown by lower-level code and caught by enclosing code. However, exceptions can occur even without using a formal exception reporting mechanism, such as when a method returns a special value indicating that it didn't complete its normal behavior. All of these forms of exceptions contribute to complexity.

A particular piece of code may encounter exceptions in several different ways:
- A caller may provide bad arguments or configuration information.
- An invoked method may not be able to complete a requested operation. For example, an I/O operation may fail, or a required resource may not be available.

- In a distributed system, network packets may be lost or delayed, servers may not respond in a timely fashion, or peers may communicate in unexpected ways.
- The code may detect bugs, internal inconsistencies, or situations it is not prepared to handle.

Large systems have to deal with many exceptional conditions, particularly if they are distributed or need to be fault-tolerant. Exception handling can account for a significant fraction of all the code in a system.

Exception handling code is inherently more difficult to write than normal-case code. An exception disrupts the normal flow of the code; it usually means that something didn't work as expected. When an exception occurs, the programmer can deal with it in two ways, each of which can be complicated. The first approach is to move forward and complete the work in progress in spite of the exception. For example, if a network packet is lost, it can be resent; if data is corrupted, perhaps it can be recovered from a redundant copy. The second approach is to abort the operation in progress and report the exception upwards. However, aborting can be complicated because the exception may have occurred at a point where system state is inconsistent (a data structure might have been partially initialized); the exception handling code must restore consistency, such as by unwinding any changes made before the exception occurred.

Furthermore, exception handling code creates opportunities for more exceptions. Consider the case of resending a lost network packet. Perhaps the packet wasn't actually lost, but was simply delayed. In this case, resending the packet will result in duplicate packets arriving at the peer; this introduces a new exceptional condition that the peer must handle. Or, consider the case of recovering lost data from a redundant copy: what if the redundant copy has also been lost? Secondary exceptions occurring during recovery are often more subtle and complex than the primary exceptions. If an exception is handled by aborting the operation in progress, then this must be reported to the caller as another exception. To prevent an unending cascade of exceptions, the developer must eventually find a way to handle exceptions without introducing more exceptions.

Language support for exceptions tends to be verbose and clunky, which makes exception handling code hard to read. For example, consider the following code, which reads a collection of tweets from a file using Java's support for object serialization and deserialization:

```
try (
    FileInputStream fileStream =
            new FileInputStream(fileName);
```

```
    BufferedInputStream bufferedStream =
            new BufferedInputStream(fileStream);
    ObjectInputStream objectStream =
            new ObjectInputStream(bufferedStream);
) {
    for (int i = 0; i < tweetsPerFile; i++) {
        tweets.add((Tweet) objectStream.readObject());
    }
}
catch (FileNotFoundException e) {
    ...
}
catch (ClassNotFoundException e) {
    ...
}
catch (EOFException e) {
    // Not a problem: not all tweet files have full
    // set of tweets.
}
catch (IOException e) {
    ...
}
catch (ClassCastException e) {
    ...
}
```

Just the basic try-catch boilerplate accounts for more lines of code than the code for normal-case operation, without even considering the code that actually handles the exceptions. It is hard to relate the exception handling code to the normal-case code: for example, it's not obvious where each exception is generated. An alternative approach is to break up the code into many distinct try blocks; in the extreme case there could be a try for each line of code that can generate an exception. This would make it clear where exceptions occur, but the try blocks themselves break up the flow of the code and make it harder to read; in addition, some exception handling code might end up duplicated in multiple try blocks.

It's difficult to ensure that exception handling code really works. Some exceptions, such as I/O errors, can't easily be generated in a test environment, so it's hard to test the code that handles them. Exceptions don't occur very often in running systems, so exception handling code rarely executes. Bugs can go undetected for a long time, and when the exception handling code is finally needed, there's a good chance that it won't work (one of my favorite sayings: "code that hasn't been executed doesn't work"). A recent study found that more than 90% of catastrophic failures in distributed data-intensive systems were caused by incorrect error handling[1]. When exception handling code fails, it's difficult to debug the problem, since it occurs so infrequently.

10.2 Too many exceptions

Programmers exacerbate the problems related to exception handling by defining unnecessary exceptions. Most programmers are taught that it's important to detect and report errors; they often interpret this to mean "the more errors detected, the better." This leads to an over-defensive style where anything that looks even a bit suspicious is rejected with an exception, which results in a proliferation of unnecessary exceptions that increase the complexity of the system.

I made this mistake myself in the design of the Tcl scripting language. Tcl contains an unset command that can be used to remove a variable. I defined unset so that it throws an error if the variable doesn't exist. At the time I thought that it must be a bug if someone tries to delete a variable that doesn't exist, so Tcl should report it. However, one of the most common uses of unset is to clean up temporary state created by some previous operation. It's often hard to predict exactly what state was created, particularly if the operation aborted partway through. Thus, the simplest thing is to delete all of the variables that might possibly have been created. The definition of unset makes this awkward: developers end up enclosing calls to unset in catch statements to catch and ignore errors thrown by unset. In retrospect, the definition of the unset command is one of the biggest mistakes I made in the design of Tcl.

It's tempting to use exceptions to avoid dealing with difficult situations: rather than figuring out a clean way to handle it, just throw an exception and punt the problem to the caller. Some might argue that this approach empowers callers, since it allows each caller to handle the exception in a different way. However, if you are having trouble figuring out what to do for the particular situation, there's a good chance that the caller won't know what to do either. Generating an exception in a situation like this just passes the problem to someone else and adds to the system's complexity.

The exceptions thrown by a class are part of its interface; **classes with lots of exceptions have complex interfaces, and they are shallower than classes with fewer exceptions**. An exception is a particularly complex element of an interface. It can

---

[1]Ding Yuan et. al., "Simple Testing Can Prevent Most Critical Failures: An Analysis of Production Failures in Distributed Data-Intensive Systems," 2014 USENIX Conference on Operating System Design and Implementation.

propagate up through several stack levels before being caught, so it affects not just the method's caller, but potentially also higher-level callers (and their interfaces).

Throwing exceptions is easy; handling them is hard. Thus, the complexity of exceptions comes from the exception handling code. The best way to reduce the complexity damage caused by exception handling is to **reduce the number of places where exceptions have to be handled**. The rest of this chapter will discuss four techniques for reducing the number of exception handlers.

10.3   Define errors out of existence

The best way to eliminate exception handling complexity is to define your APIs so that there are no exceptions to handle: **define errors out of existence**. This may seem sacrilegious, but it is very effective in practice. Consider the Tcl unset command discussed above. Rather than throwing an error when unset is asked to delete an unknown variable, it should have simply returned without doing anything. I should have changed the definition of unset slightly: rather than deleting a variable, unset should ensure that a variable no longer exists. With the first definition, unset can't do its job if the variable doesn't exist, so generating an exception makes sense. With the second definition, it is perfectly natural for unset to be invoked with the name of a variable that doesn't exist. In this case, its work is already done, so it can simply return. There is no longer an error case to report.

10.4   Example: file deletion in Windows

File deletion provides another example of how errors can be defined away. The Windows operating system does not permit a file to be deleted if it is open in a process. This is a continual source of frustration for developers and users. In order to delete a file that is in use, the user must search through the system to find the process that has the file open, and then kill that process. Sometimes users give up and reboot their system, just so they can delete a file.

The Unix operating system defines file deletion more elegantly. In Unix, if a file is open when it is deleted, Unix does not delete the file immediately. Instead, it marks the file for deletion, then the delete operation returns successfully. The file name has been removed from its directory, so no other processes can open the old file and a new file with the same name can be created, but the existing file data persists. Processes that already have the file open can continue to read it and write it normally. Once the file has been closed by all of the accessing processes, its data is freed.

The Unix approach defines away two different kinds of errors. First, the delete operation no longer returns an error if the file is currently in use; the delete succeeds, and the file will eventually be deleted. Second, deleting a file that's in use does not create exceptions for the processes using the file. One possible approach to this problem would have been to delete the file immediately and mark all of the opens of the file to disable them; any attempts by other processes to read or write the deleted file would fail. However, this approach would create new errors for those processes to handle. Instead, Unix allows them to keep accessing the file normally; delaying the file deletion defines errors out of existence.

It may seem strange that Unix allows a process to continue to read and write a doomed file, but I have never encountered a situation where this caused significant problems. The Unix definition of file deletion is much simpler to work with, both for developers and users, than the Windows definition.

10.5   Example: Java substring method

As a final example, consider the Java `String` class and its `substring` method. Given two indexes into a string, `substring` returns the substring starting at the character given by the first index and ending with the character just before the second index. However, if either index is outside the range of the string, then `substring` throws `IndexOutOfBoundsException`. This exception is unnecessary and complicates the use of this method. I often find myself in a situation where one or both of the indices may be outside the range of the string, and I would like to extract all of the characters in the string that overlap the specified range. Unfortunately, this requires me to check each of the indices and round them up to zero or down to the end of the string; a one-line method call now becomes 5–10 lines of code.

The Java `substring` method would be easier to use if it performed this adjustment automatically, so that it implemented the following API: "returns the characters of the string (if any) with index greater than or equal to `beginIndex` and less than `endIndex`." This is a simple and natural API, and it defines the `IndexOutOfBounds-Exception` exception out of existence. The method's behavior is now well-defined even if one or both of the indexes are negative, or if `beginIndex` is greater than `endIndex`. This approach simplifies the API for the method while increasing its functionality, so it makes the method deeper. Many other languages have taken the error-free approach; for example, Python returns an empty result for out-of-range list slices.

When I argue for defining errors out of existence, people sometimes counter that throwing errors will catch bugs; if errors are defined out of existence, won't that result in buggier software? Perhaps this is why the Java developers decided that substring should throw exceptions. The error-ful approach may catch some bugs, but it also increases complexity, which results in other bugs. In the error-ful approach, developers must write additional code to avoid or ignore the errors, and this increases the likelihood of bugs; or, they may forget to write the additional code, in which case unexpected errors may be thrown at runtime. In contrast, defining errors out of existence simplifies APIs and it reduces the amount of code that must be written.

Overall, the best way to reduce bugs is to make software simpler.

10.6 Mask exceptions

The second technique for reducing the number of places where exceptions must be handled is *exception masking*. With this approach, an exceptional condition is detected and handled at a low level in the system, so that higher levels of software need not be aware of the condition. Exception masking is particularly common in distributed systems. For instance, in a network transport protocol such as TCP, packets can be dropped for various reasons such as corruption and congestion. TCP masks packet loss by resending lost packets within its implementation, so all data eventually gets through and clients are unaware of the dropped packets.

A more controversial example of masking occurs in the NFS network file system. If an NFS file server crashes or fails to respond for any reason, clients reissue their requests to the server over and over again until the problem is eventually resolved. The low-level file system code on the client does not report any exceptions to the invoking application. The operation in progress (and hence the application) just hangs until the operation can complete successfully. If the hang lasts more than a short time, the NFS client prints messages on the user's console of the form "NFS server xyzzy not responding still trying."

NFS users often complain about the fact that their applications hang while waiting for an NFS server to resume normal operation. Many people have suggested that NFS should abort operations with an exception rather than hanging. However, reporting exceptions would make things worse, not better. There's not much an application can do if it loses access to its files. One possibility would be for the application to retry the file operation, but this would still hang the application, and it's easier to perform the retry in one place in the NFS layer, rather than at every file system call in every application (a compiler shouldn't have to worry about this!). The other alternative is for applications to abort and return errors to their callers. It's unlikely that the callers would know what to do either, so they would abort as well, resulting in a collapse of the user's working environment. Users still wouldn't be able to get any work done while the file server was down, and they would have to restart all of their applications once the file server came back to life.

Thus, the best alternative is for NFS to mask the errors and hang applications. With this approach, applications don't need any code to deal with server problems, and they can resume seamlessly once the server comes back to life. If users get tired of waiting, they can always abort applications manually.

Exception masking doesn't work in all situations, but it is a powerful tool in the situations where it works. It results in deeper classes, since it reduces the class's interface (fewer exceptions for users to be aware of) and adds functionality in the form of the code that masks the exception. Exception masking is an example of pulling complexity downward.

10.7 Exception aggregation

The third technique for reducing complexity related to exceptions is *exception aggregation*. The idea behind exception aggregation is to handle many exceptions with a single piece of code; rather than writing distinct handlers for many individual exceptions, handle them all in one place with a single handler.

Consider how to handle missing parameters in a Web server. A Web server implements a collection of URLs. When the server receives an incoming URL, it dispatches to a URL-specific service method to process that URL and generate a response. The URL contains various parameters that are used to generate the response. Each service method will call a lower-level method (let's call it getParameter) to extract the parameters that it needs from the URL. If the URL does not contain the desired parameter, getParameter throws an exception.

When students in a software design class implemented such a server, many of them wrapped each distinct call to getParameter in a separate exception handler to catch NoSuchParameter exceptions, as in Figure 10.1. This resulted in a large number of handlers, all of which did essentially the same thing (generate an error response).

82

Dispatcher:

```
...
if (...) {
    handleUrl1(...);
} else if (...) {
    handleUrl2(...);
} else if (...) {
    handleUrl3(...);
} else if (...)
    ...
}
...
```

handleUrl1:

```
...
try {
    ... getParameter("photo_id")
    ...
} catch (NoSuchParameter e) {
    ...
}
...
try {
    ... getParameter("message")
    ...
} catch (NoSuchParameter e) {
    ...
}
...
```

handleUrl2:

```
...
try {
    ... getParameter("user_id")
    ...
} catch (NoSuchParameter e) {
    ...
}
...
```

handleUrl3:

```
...
try {
    ... getParameter("login")
    ...
} catch (NoSuchParameter e) {
    ...
}
...
try {
    ... getParameter("password")
    ...
} catch (NoSuchParameter e) {
    ...
}
...
```

Figure 10.1: The code at the top dispatches to one of several methods in a Web server, each of which handles a particular URL. Each of those methods (bottom) uses parameters from the incoming HTTP request. In this figure, there is a separate exception handler for each call to getParameter; this results in duplicated code.

A better approach is to aggregate the exceptions. Instead of catching the exceptions in the individual service methods, let them propagate up to the top-level dispatch method for the Web server, as in Figure 10.2. A single handler in this method can catch all of the exceptions and generate an appropriate error response for missing parameters.

The aggregation approach can be taken even further in the Web example. There are many other errors besides missing parameters that can occur while processing a Web page; for example, a parameter might not have the right syntax (the service method expected an integer, but the value was "xyz"), or the user might not have permission for the requested operation. In each case, the error should result in an error response; the

Dispatcher:

```
...
try {
  if (...) {
    handleUrl1(...);
  } else if (...) {
    handleUrl2(...);
  } else if (...) {
    handleUrl3(...);
  } else if (...)
    ...
  }
} catch (NoSuchParameter e) {
  send error response;
}
...
```

handleUrl1:

```
... getParameter("photo_id")
... getParameter("message")
...
```

handleUrl2:

```
... getParameter("user_id")
...
```

handleUrl3:

```
... getParameter("login")
... getParameter("password")
...
```

Figure 10.2: This code is functionally equivalent to Figure 10.1, but exception handling has been aggregated: a single exception handler in the dispatcher catches all of the NoSuchParameter exceptions from all of the URL-specific methods.

errors differ only in the error message to include in the response ("parameter 'quantity' not present in URL" or "bad value 'xyz' for 'quantity' parameter; must be positive integer"). Thus, all conditions resulting in an error response can be handled with a single top-level exception handler. The error message can be generated at the time the exception is thrown and included as a variable in the exception record; for example, getParameter will generate the "parameter 'quantity' not present in URL" message. The top-level handler extracts the message from the exception and incorporates it into the error response.

The aggregation described in the preceding paragraph has good properties from the standpoint of encapsulation and information hiding. The top-level exception handler encapsulates knowledge about how to generate error responses, but it knows nothing about specific errors; it just uses the error message provided in the exception. The getParameter method encapsulates knowledge about how to extract a parameter from a URL, and it also knows how to describe extraction errors in a human-readable form. These two pieces of information are closely related, so it makes sense for them to be in the same place. However, getParameter knows nothing about the syntax of

84

an HTTP error response. As new functionality is added to the Web server, new methods like getParameter may be created with their own errors. If the new methods throw exceptions in the same way as getParameter (by generating exceptions that inherit from the same superclass and including an error message in each exception), they can plug into the existing system with no other changes: the top-level handler will automatically generate error responses for them.

This example illustrates a generally-useful design pattern for exception handling. If a system processes a series of requests, it's useful to define an exception that aborts the current request, cleans up the system's state, and continues with the next request. The exception is caught in a single place near the top of the system's request-handling loop. This exception can be thrown at any point in the processing of a request to abort the request; different subclasses of the exception can be defined for different conditions. Exceptions of this type should be clearly distinguished from exceptions that are fatal to the entire system.

Exception aggregation works best if an exception propagates several levels up the stack before it is handled; this allows more exceptions from more methods to be handled in the same place. This is the opposite of exception masking: masking usually works best if an exception is handled in a low-level method. For masking, the low-level method is typically a library method used by many other methods, so allowing the exception to propagate would increase the number of places where it is handled. Masking and aggregation are similar in that both approaches position an exception handler where it can catch the most exceptions, eliminating many handlers that would otherwise need to be created.

Another example of exception aggregation occurs in the RAMCloud storage system for crash recovery. A RAMCloud system consists of a collection of storage servers that keep multiple copies of each object, so the system can recover from a variety of failures. For example, if a server crashes and loses all of its data, RAMCloud reconstructs the lost data using copies stored on other servers. Errors can also happen on a smaller scale; for example, a server may discover that an individual object is corrupted.

RAMCloud does not have separate recovery mechanisms for each different kind of error. Instead, RAMCloud "promotes" many smaller errors into larger ones. RAMCloud could, in principle, handle a corrupted object by restoring that one object from a backup copy. However, it doesn't do this. Instead, if it discovers a corrupted object it crashes the server containing the object. RAMCloud uses this approach because crash recovery is quite complex and this approach minimized the number of different recovery mechanisms that had to be created. Creating a recovery mechanism for crashed servers was unavoidable, so RAMCloud uses the same mechanism for other kinds of recovery as well. This reduced the amount of code that had to be written, and it also meant that server crash recovery gets invoked more often. As a result, bugs in recovery are more likely to be discovered and fixed.

One disadvantage of promoting a corrupted object into a server crash is that it increases the cost of recovery considerably. This is not a problem in RAMCloud, since object corruption is quite rare. However, error promotion may not make sense for errors that happen frequently. As one example, it would not be practical to crash a server anytime one of its network packets is lost.

One way of thinking about exception aggregation is that it replaces several special-purpose mechanisms, each tailored for a particular situation, with a single general-purpose mechanism that can handle multiple situations. This provides another illustration of the benefits of general-purpose mechanisms.

10.8 Just crash?

The fourth technique for reducing complexity related to exception handling is to crash the application. In most applications there will be certain errors that it's not worth trying to handle. Typically, these errors are difficult or impossible to handle and don't occur very often. The simplest thing to do in response to these errors is to print diagnostic information and then abort the application.

One example is "out of memory" errors that occur during storage allocation. Consider the malloc function in C, which returns NULL if it cannot allocate the desired block of memory. This is an unfortunate behavior, because it assumes that every single caller of malloc will check the return value and take appropriate action if there is no memory. Applications contain numerous calls to malloc, so checking the result after each call would add significant complexity. If a programmer forgets the check (which is fairly likely), then the application will dereference a null pointer if memory runs out, resulting in a crash that camouflages the real problem.

Furthermore, there isn't much an application can do when it discovers that memory is exhausted. In principle the application could look for unneeded memory to free, but if the application had unneeded memory it could already have freed it, which would have prevented the out-of-memory error in the first place. Today's systems have so much memory that memory almost never runs out; if it does, it usually indicates a bug in the application. Thus, it rarely make sense to try to handle out-of-memory errors; this creates too much complexity for too little benefit.

A better approach is to define a new method ckalloc, which calls malloc, checks the result, and aborts the application with an error message if memory is exhausted. The application never invokes malloc directly; it always invokes ckalloc.

In newer languages such as C++ and Java, the new operator throws an exception if memory is exhausted. There's not much point in catching this exception, since there's a good chance that the exception handler will also try to allocate memory, which will also fail. Dynamically allocated memory is such a fundamental element of any modern application that it doesn't make sense for the application to continue if memory is exhausted; it's better to crash as soon as the error is detected.

There are many other examples of errors where crashing the application makes sense. For most programs, if an I/O error occurs while reading or writing an open file (such as a disk hard error), or if a network socket cannot be opened, there's not much the application can do to recover, so aborting with a clear error message is a sensible approach. These errors are infrequent, so they are unlikely to affect the overall usability of the application. Aborting with an error message is also appropriate if an application encounters an internal error such as an inconsistent data structure. Conditions like this probably indicate bugs in the program.

Whether or not it is acceptable to crash on a particular error depends on the application. For a replicated storage system, it isn't appropriate to abort on an I/O error. Instead, the system must use replicated data to recover any information that was lost. The recovery mechanisms will add considerable complexity to the program, but recovering lost data is an essential part of the value the system provides to its users.

10.9   Design special cases out of existence

For the same reason that it makes sense to define errors out of existence, it also makes sense to define other special cases out of existence. Special cases can result in code that is riddled with if statements, which make the code hard to understand and lead to bugs. Thus, special cases should be eliminated wherever possible. The best way to do this is by designing the normal case in a way that automatically handles the special cases without any extra code.

In the text editor project described in Chapter 6, students had to implement a mechanism for selecting text and copying or deleting the selection. Most students introduced a state variable in their selection implementation to indicate whether or not the selection exists. They probably chose this approach because there are times when no selection is visible on the screen, so it seemed natural to represent this notion in the implementation. However, this approach resulted in numerous checks to detect the "no selection" condition and handle it specially.

The selection handling code can be simplified by eliminating the "no selection" special case, so that the selection always exists. When there is no selection visible on the screen, it can be represented internally with an empty selection, whose starting and ending positions are the same. With this approach, the selection management code can be written without any checks for "no selection". When copying the selection, if the selection is empty then 0 bytes will be inserted at the new location (if implemented correctly, there will be no need to check for 0 bytes as a special case). Similarly, it should be possible to design the code for deleting the selection so that the empty case is handled without any special-case checks. Consider a selection all on a single line. To delete the selection, extract the portion of the line preceding the selection and concatenate it with the portion of the line following the selection to form the new line. If the selection is empty, this approach will regenerate the original line.

This example also illustrates the "different layer, different abstraction" idea from Chapter 7. The notion of "no selection" makes sense in terms of how the user thinks about the application's interface, but that doesn't mean it has to be represented explicitly inside the application. Having a selection that always exists, but is sometimes empty and thus invisible, results in a simpler implementation.

10.10   Taking it too far

Defining away exceptions, or masking them inside a module, only makes sense if the exception information isn't needed outside the module. This was true for the examples in this chapter, such the Tcl unset command and the Java substring method; in the rare situations where a caller cares about the special cases detected by the exceptions, there are other ways for it to get this information.

However, it is possible to take this idea too far. In a module for network communication, a student team masked all network exceptions: if a network error occurred, the module caught it, discarded it, and continued as if there were no problem. This meant that applications using the module had no way to find out if messages were lost or a peer server failed; without this information, it was impossible to build robust applications. In this case, it is essential for the module to expose the exceptions, even though they add complexity to the module's interface.

With exceptions, as with many other areas in software design, you must determine what is important and what is not important. Things that are not important should be hidden, and the more of them the better. But when something is important, it must be exposed.

10.11 Conclusion

Special cases of any form make code harder to understand and increase the likelihood of bugs. This chapter focused on exceptions, which are one of the most significant sources of special-case code, and discussed how to reduce the number of places where exceptions must be handled. The best way to do this is by redefining semantics to eliminate error conditions. For exceptions that can't be defined away, you should look for opportunities to mask them at a low level, so their impact is limited, or aggregate several special-case handlers into a single more generic handler. Together, these techniques can have a significant impact on overall system complexity.

Chapter 11

Design it Twice

Designing software is hard, so it's unlikely that your first thoughts about how to structure a module or system will produce the best design. You'll end up with a much better result if you consider multiple options for each major design decision: **design it twice**.

Suppose you are designing the class that will manage the text of a file for a GUI text editor. The first step is to define the interface that the class will present to the rest of the editor; rather than picking the first idea that comes to mind, consider several possibilities. One choice is a line-oriented interface, with operations to insert, modify, and delete whole lines of text. Another option is an interface based on individual character insertions and deletions. A third choice is a string-oriented interface, which operates on arbitrary ranges of characters that may cross line boundaries. You don't need to pin down every feature of each alternative; it's sufficient at this point to sketch out a few of the most important methods.

Try to pick approaches that are radically different from each other; you'll learn more that way. Even if you are certain that there is only one reasonable approach, consider a second design anyway, no matter how bad you think it will be. It will be instructive to think about the weaknesses of that design and contrast them with the features of other designs.

After you have roughed out the designs for the alternatives, make a list of the pros and cons of each one. The most important consideration for an interface is ease of use for higher level software. In the example above, both the line-oriented interface and the character-oriented interface will require extra work in software that uses the text class. The line-oriented interface will require higher level software to split and join lines during partial-line and multi-line operations such as cutting and pasting the selection. The character-oriented interface will require loops to implement operations

91

that modify more than a single character. It is also worth considering other factors:

- Does one alternative have a simpler interface than another? In the text example, all of the text interfaces are relatively simple.
- Is one interface more general-purpose than another?
- Does one interface enable a more efficient implementation than another? In the text example, the character-oriented approach is likely to be significantly slower than the others, because it requires a separate call into the text module for each character.

Once you have compared alternative designs, you will be in a better position to identify the best design. The best choice may be one of the alternatives, or you may discover that you can combine features of multiple alternatives into a new design that is better than any of the original choices.

Sometimes none of the alternatives is particularly attractive; when this happens, see if you can come up with additional schemes. Use the problems you identified with the original alternatives to drive the new design(s). If you were designing the text class and considered only the line-oriented and character-oriented approaches, you might notice that each of the alternatives is awkward because it requires higher level software to perform additional text manipulations. That's a red flag: if there's going to be a text class, it should handle all of the text manipulation. In order to eliminate the additional text manipulations, the text interface needs to match more closely the operations happening in higher level software. These operations don't always correspond to single characters or single lines. This line of reasoning should lead you to a range-oriented API for text, which eliminates the problem with the earlier designs.

The design-it-twice principle can be applied at many levels in a system. For a module, you can use this approach first to pick the interface, as described above. Then you can apply it again when you are designing the implementation: for the text class, you might consider implementations such as a linked list of lines, fixed-size blocks of characters, or a "gap buffer." The goals will be different for the implementation than for the interface: for the implementation, the most important things are simplicity and performance. It's also useful to explore multiple designs at higher levels in the system, such as when choosing features for a user interface, or when decomposing a system into major modules. In each case, it's easier to identify the best approach if you can compare a few alternatives.

Designing it twice does not need to take a lot of extra time. For a smaller module such as a class, you may not need more than an hour or two to consider alternatives. This is a small amount of time compared to the days or weeks you will spend implementing the class. The initial design experiments will probably result in a significantly better design, which will more than pay for the time spent designing it twice. For larger modules you'll spend more time in the in the initial design explorations, but the implementation will also take longer, and the benefits of a better design will also be higher.

I have noticed that the design-it-twice principle is sometimes hard for really smart people to embrace. When they are growing up, smart people discover that their first quick idea about any problem is sufficient for a good grade; there is no need to consider a second or third possibility. This makes it easy to develop bad work habits. However, as these people get older, they get promoted into environments with harder and harder problems. Eventually, everyone reaches a point where your first ideas are no longer good enough; if you want to get really great results, you have to consider a second possibility, or perhaps a third, no matter how smart you are. The design of large software systems falls in this category: no-one is good enough to get it right with their first try.

Unfortunately, I often see smart people who insist on implementing the first idea that comes to mind, and this causes them to underperform their true potential (it also makes them frustrating to work with). Perhaps they subconsciously believe that "smart people get it right the first time," so if they try multiple designs it would mean they are not smart after all. This is not the case. It isn't that you aren't smart; it's that the problems are really hard! Furthermore, that's a good thing: it's much more fun to work on a difficult problem where you have to think carefully, rather than an easy problem where you don't have to think at all.

The design-it-twice approach not only improves your designs, but it also improves your design skills. The process of devising and comparing multiple approaches will teach you about the factors that make designs better or worse. Over time, this will make it easier for you to rule out bad designs and hone in on really great ones.

93

Chapter 12

Why Write Comments? The Four Excuses

In-code documentation plays a crucial role in software design. Comments are essential to help developers understand a system and work efficiently, but the role of comments goes beyond this. Documentation also plays an important role in abstraction; without comments, you can't hide complexity. Finally, **the process of writing comments, if done correctly, will actually improve a system's design.** Conversely, a good software design loses much of its value if it is poorly documented.

Unfortunately, this view is not universally shared. A significant fraction of production code contains essentially no comments. Many developers think that comments are a waste of time; others see the value in comments, but somehow never get around to writing them. Fortunately, many development teams recognize the value of documentation, and it feels like the prevalence of these teams is gradually increasing. However, even in teams that encourage documentation, comments are often viewed as drudge work and many developers don't understand how to write them, so the resulting documentation is often mediocre. Inadequate documentation creates a huge and unnecessary drag on software development.

In this chapter I will discuss the excuses developers use to avoid writing comments, and the reasons why comments really do matter. Chapter 13 will then describe how to write good comments and the next few chapters after that will discuss related issues such as choosing variable names and how to use documentation to improve a system's design. I hope these chapters will convince you of three things: good comments can make a big difference in the overall quality of software; it isn't hard to write good comments; and (this may be hard to believe) writing comments can actually be fun.

When developers don't write comments, they usually justify their behavior with one or more of the following excuses:
- "Good code is self-documenting."
- "I don't have time to write comments."
- "Comments get out of date and become misleading."
- "The comments I have seen are all worthless; why bother?"

In the sections below I will address each of these excuses in turn.

12.1   Good code is self-documenting

Some people believe that if code is written well, it is so obvious that no comments are needed. This is a delicious myth, like a rumor that ice cream is good for your health: we'd really like to believe it! Unfortunately, it's simply not true. To be sure, there are things you can do when writing code to reduce the need for comments, such as choosing good variable names (see Chapter 14). Nonetheless, there is still a significant amount of design information that can't be represented in code. For example, only a small part of a class's interface, such as the signatures of its methods, can be specified formally in the code. The informal aspects of an interface, such as a high-level description of what each method does or the meaning of its result, can only be described in comments. There are many other examples of things that can't be described in the code, such as the rationale for a particular design decision, or the conditions under which it makes sense to call a particular method.

Some developers argue that if others want to know what a method does, they should just read the code of the method: this will be more accurate than any comment. It's possible that a reader could deduce the abstract interface of the method by reading its code, but it would be time-consuming and painful. In addition, if you write code with the expectation that users will read method implementations, you will try to make each method as short as possible, so that it's easy to read. If the method does anything nontrivial, you will break it up into several smaller methods. This will result in a large number of shallow methods. Furthermore, it doesn't really make the code easier to read: in order to understand the behavior of the top-level method, readers will probably need to understand the behaviors of the nested methods. For large systems it isn't practical for users to read the code to learn the behavior.

Moreover, comments are fundamental to abstractions. Recall from Chapter 4 that the goal of abstractions is to hide complexity: an abstraction is a simplified view of an entity, which preserves essential information but omits details that can safely be ignored. **If users must read the code of a method in order to use it, then there is no abstraction**: all of the complexity of the method is exposed. Without comments, the only abstraction of a method is its declaration, which specifies its name and the names and types of its arguments and results. The declaration is missing too much essential information to provide a useful abstraction by itself. For example, a method to extract a substring might have two arguments, `start` and `end`, indicating the range of characters to extract. From the declaration alone, it isn't possible to tell whether the extracted substring will include the character indicated by `end`, or what happens if `start` > `end`. Comments allow us to capture the additional information that callers need, thereby completing the simplified view while hiding implementation details. It's also important that comments are written in a human language such as English; this makes them less precise than code, but it provides more expressive power, so we can create simple, intuitive descriptions. If you want to use abstractions to hide complexity, comments are essential.

12.2   I don't have time to write comments

It's tempting to prioritize comments lower than other development tasks. Given a choice between adding a new feature and documenting an existing feature, it seems logical to choose the new feature. However, software projects are almost always under time pressure, and there will always be things that seem higher priority than writing comments. Thus, if you allow documentation to be de-prioritized, you'll end up with no documentation.

The counter-argument to this excuse is the investment mindset discussed on page 15. If you want a clean software structure, which will allow you to work efficiently over the long-term, then you must take some extra time up front in order to create that structure. Good comments make a huge difference in the maintainability of software, so the effort spent on them will pay for itself quickly. Furthermore, writing comments needn't take a lot of time. Ask yourself how much of your development time you spend typing in code (as opposed to designing, compiling, testing, etc.), assuming you don't include any comments; I doubt that the answer is more than 10%. Now suppose that you spend as much time typing comments as typing code; this should be a safe upper bound. With these assumptions, writing good comments won't add more than about 10% to your development time. The benefits of having good documentation will quickly offset this cost.

Furthermore, many of the most important comments are those related to abstractions, such as the top-level documentation for classes and methods. Chapter 15 will argue that these comments should be written as part of the design process, and that the act of writing the documentation serves as an important design tool that improves the overall design. These comments pay for themselves immediately.

12.3 Comments get out of date and become misleading

Comments do sometimes get out of date, but this need not be a major problem in practice. Keeping documentation up-to-date does not require an enormous effort. Large changes to the documentation are only required if there have been large changes to the code, and the code changes will take more time than the documentation changes. Chapter 16 discusses how to organize documentation so that it is as easy as possible to keep it updated after code modifications (the key ideas are to avoid duplicated documentation and keep the documentation close to the corresponding code). Code reviews provide a great mechanism for detecting and fixing stale comments.

12.4 All the comments I have seen are worthless

Of the four excuses, this is probably the one with the most merit. Every software developer has seen comments that provide no useful information, and most existing documentation is so-so at best. Fortunately, this problem is solvable; writing solid documentation is not hard, once you know how. The next chapters will lay out a framework for how to write good documentation and maintain it over time.

12.5 Benefits of well-written comments

Now that I have discussed (and, hopefully, debunked) the arguments against writing comments, let's consider the benefits that you will get from good comments. **The overall idea behind comments is to capture information that was in the mind of the designer but couldn't be represented in the code.** This information ranges from low-level details, such as a hardware quirk that motivates a particularly tricky piece of code, up to high-level concepts such as the rationale for a class. When other developers come along later to make modifications, the comments will allow them to work more quickly and accurately. Without documentation, future developers will have to re-derive or guess at the developer's original knowledge; this will take additional time, and there is a risk of bugs if the new developer misunderstands the original designer's intentions. Comments are valuable even when the original designer is the one making the changes: if it has been more than a few weeks since you last worked in a piece of code, you will have forgotten many of the details of the original design.

Chapter 2 described three ways in which complexity manifests itself in software systems:

Change amplification: a seemingly simple change requires code modifications in many places.

Cognitive load: in order to make a change, the developer must accumulate a large amount of information.

Unknown unknowns: it is unclear what code needs to be modified, or what information must be considered in order to make those modifications.

Good documentation helps with the last two of these issues. Documentation can reduce cognitive load by providing developers with the information they need to make changes and by making it easy for developers to ignore information that is irrelevant. Without adequate documentation, developers may have to read large amounts of code to reconstruct what was in the designer's mind. Documentation can also reduce the unknown unknowns by clarifying the structure of the system, so that it is clear what information and code is relevant for any given change.

Chapter 2 pointed out that the primary causes of complexity are dependencies and obscurity. Good documentation can clarify dependencies, and it fills in gaps to eliminate obscurity.

The next few chapters will show you how to write good documentation. They will also discuss how to integrate documentation-writing into the design process so that it improves the design of your software.

Chapter 13

Comments Should Describe Things that Aren't Obvious from the Code

The reason for writing comments is that statements in a programming language can't capture all of the important information that was in the mind of the developer when the code was written. Comments record this information so that developers who come along later can easily understand and modify the code. The guiding principle for comments is that **comments should describe things that aren't obvious from the code**.

There are many things that aren't obvious from the code. Sometimes it's low-level details that aren't obvious. For example, when a pair of indices describe a range, it isn't obvious whether the elements given by the indices are inside the range or out. Sometimes it's not clear why code is needed, or why it was implemented in a particular way. Sometimes there are rules the developer followed, such as "always invoke a before b." You might be able to guess at a rule by looking at all of the code, but this is painful and error-prone; a comment can make the rule explicit and clear.

One of the most important reasons for comments is abstractions, which include a lot of information that isn't obvious from the code. The idea of an abstraction is to provide a simple way of thinking about something, but code is so detailed that it can be hard to see the abstraction just from reading the code. Comments can provide a simpler, higher-level view ("after this method is invoked, network traffic will be limited to maxBandwidth bytes per second"). Even if this information can be deduced by reading the code, we don't want to force users of a module to do that: reading the code is time-consuming and forces them to consider a lot of information that isn't needed to use the module. **Developers should be able to understand the abstraction provided by a module without reading any code other than its externally visible declarations.** The only way to do this is by supplementing the declarations with comments.

This chapter discusses what information needs to be described in comments and how to write good comments. As you will see, good comments typically explain things at a different level of detail than the code, which is more detailed in some situations and less detailed (more abstract) in others.

13.1   Pick conventions

The first step in writing comments is to decide on conventions for commenting, such as what you will comment and the format you will use for comments. If you are programming in a language for which there exists a document compilation tool, such as Javadoc for Java, Doxygen for C++, or godoc for Go!, follow the conventions of the tools. None of these conventions is perfect, but the tools provide enough benefits to make up for that. If you are programming in an environment where there are no existing conventions to follow, try to adopt the conventions from some other language or project that is similar; this will make it easier for other developers to understand and adhere to your conventions.

Conventions serve two purposes. First, they ensure consistency, which makes comments easier to read and understand. Second, they help to ensure that you actually write comments. If you don't have a clear idea what you are going to comment and how, it's easy to end up writing no comments at all.

Most comments fall into one of the following categories:

Interface: a comment block that immediately precedes the declaration of a module such as a class, data structure, function, or method. The comment describe's the module's interface. For a class, the comment describes the overall abstraction provided by the class. For a method or function, the comment describes its overall behavior, its arguments and return value, if any, any side effects or exceptions that it generates, and any other requirements the caller must satisfy before invoking the method.

Data structure member: a comment next to the declaration of a field in a data structure, such as an instance variable or static variable for a class.

Implementation comment: a comment inside the code of a method or function, which describes how the code works internally.

Cross-module comment: a comment describing dependencies that cross module boundaries.

The most important comments are those in the first two categories. Every class should have an interface comment, every class variable should have a comment, and every method should have an interface comment Occasionally, the declaration for a variable or method is so obvious that there is nothing useful to add in a comment (getters and setters sometimes fall in this category), but this is rare; it is easier to comment everything rather than spend energy worrying about whether a comment is needed. Implementation comments are often unnecessary (see Section 13.6 below). Cross-module comments are the most rare of all and they are problematic to write, but when they are needed they are quite important; Section 13.7 discusses them in more detail.

13.2 Don't repeat the code

Unfortunately, many comments are not particularly helpful. The most common reason is that the comments repeat the code: all of the information in the comment can easily be deduced from the code next to the comment. Here is a code sample that appeared in a recent research paper:

```
ptr_copy = get_copy(obj)          # Get pointer copy
if is_unlocked(ptr_copy):         # Is obj free?
    return obj                    # return current obj
if is_copy(ptr_copy):             # Already a copy?
    return obj                    # return obj
thread_id = get_thread_id(ptr_copy)
if thread_id == ctx.thread_id:    # Locked by current ctx
    return ptr_copy               # Return copy
```

There is no useful information in any of these comments except for the "Locked by" comment, which suggests something about the thread that might not be obvious from the code. Notice that these comments are at roughly the same level of detail as the code: there is one comment per line of code, which describes that line. Comments like this are rarely useful.

Here are more examples of comments that repeat the code:

```
// Add a horizontal scroll bar
hScrollBar = new JScrollBar(JScrollBar.HORIZONTAL);
add(hScrollBar, BorderLayout.SOUTH);

// Add a vertical scroll bar
vScrollBar = new JScrollBar(JScrollBar.VERTICAL);
```

103

```
add(vScrollBar, BorderLayout.EAST);

// Initialize the caret-position related values
caretX    = 0;
caretY    = 0;
caretMemX = null;
```

None of these comments provide any value. For the first two comments, the code is already clear enough that it doesn't really need comments; in the third case, a comment might be useful, but the current comment doesn't provide enough detail to be helpful.

After you have written a comment, ask yourself the following question: could someone who has never seen the code write the comment just by looking at the code next to the comment? If the answer is yes, as in the examples above, then the comment doesn't make the code any easier to understand. Comments like these are why some people think that comments are worthless.

Another common mistake is to use the same words in the comment that appear in the name of the entity being documented:

```
/*
 * Obtain a normalized resource name from REQ.
 */
private static String[] getNormalizedResourceNames(
        HTTPRequest req) ...

/*
 * Downcast PARAMETER to TYPE.
 */
private static Object downCastParameter(String parameter,
        String type) ...

/*
 * The horizontal padding of each line in the text.
 */
```

 Red Flag: Comment Repeats Code

If the information in a comment is already obvious from the code next to the comment, then the comment isn't helpful. One example of this is when the comment uses the same words that make up the name of the thing it is describing.

```
private static final int textHorizontalPadding = 4;
```

These comments just take the words from the method or variable name, perhaps add a few words from argument names and types, and form them into a sentence. For example, the only thing in the second comment that isn't in the code is the word "to"! Once again, these comments could be written just by looking at the declarations, without any understanding the methods of variables; as a result, they have no value.

At the same time, there is important information that is missing from the comments: for example, what is a "normalized resource name", and what are the elements of the array returned by getNormalizedResourceNames? What does "downcast" mean? What are the units of padding, and is the padding on one side of each line or both? Describing these things in comments would be helpful.

A first step towards writing good comments is to **use different words in the comment from those in the name of the entity being described.** Pick words for the comment that provide additional information about the meaning of the entity, rather than just repeating its name. For example, here is a better comment for textHorizontal-Padding:

```
/*
 * The amount of blank space to leave on the left and
 * right sides of each line of text, in pixels.
 */
private static final int textHorizontalPadding = 4;
```

This comment provides additional information that is not obvious from the declaration itself, such as the units (pixels) and the fact that padding applies to both sides of each line. Instead of using the term "padding", the comment explains what padding is, in case the reader isn't already familiar with the term.

13.3   Lower-level comments add precision

Now that you know what not to do, let's discuss what information you *should* put in comments. **Comments augment the code by providing information at a different level of detail.** Some comments provide information at a lower, more detailed, level than the code; these comments add *precision* by clarifying the exact meaning of the code. Other comments provide information at a higher, more abstract, level than the code; these comments offer *intuition*, such as the reasoning behind the code, or a simpler and more abstract way of thinking about the code. Comments at the same level as the code are likely to repeat the code. This section discusses the lower-level approach in more detail, and the next section discusses the higher-level approach.

Precision is most useful when commenting variable declarations such as class instance variables, method arguments, and return values. The name and type in a variable declaration are typically not very precise. Comments can fill in missing details such as:

- What are the units for this variable?
- Are the boundary conditions inclusive or exclusive?
- If a null value is permitted, what does it imply?
- If a variable refers to a resource that must eventually be freed or closed, who is responsible for freeing or closing it?
- Are there certain properties that are always true for the variable (*invariants*), such as "this list always contains at least one entry"?

Some of this information could potentially be figured out by examining all of the code where the variable is used. However, this is time-consuming and error-prone; the declaration's comment should be clear and complete enough to make this unnecessary. When I say that the comment for a declaration should describe things that aren't obvious from the code, "the code" refers to the code next to the comment (the declaration), not "all of the code in the application."

The most common problem with comments for variables is that the comments are too vague. Here are two examples of comments that aren't precise enough:

```
// Current offset in resp Buffer
uint32_t offset;

// Contains all line-widths inside the document and
// number of appearances.
private TreeMap<Integer, Integer> lineWidths;
```

In the first example, it's not clear what "current" means. In the second example, it's not clear that the keys in the TreeMap are line widths and values are occurrence counts. Also, are widths measured in pixels or characters? The revised comments below provide additional details:

```
// Position in this buffer of the first object that hasn't
// been returned to the client.
uint32_t offset;

// Holds statistics about line lengths of the form <length, count>
// where length is the number of characters in a line (including
// the newline), and count is the number of lines with
// exactly that many characters. If there are no lines with
```

```
// a particular length, then there is no entry for that length.
private TreeMap<Integer, Integer> numLinesWithLength;
```

The second declaration uses a longer name that conveys more information. It also changes "width" to "length", because this term is more likely to make people think that the units are characters rather than pixels. Notice that the second comment documents not only the details of each entry, but also what it means if an entry is missing.

When documenting a variable, think *nouns*, not *verbs*. In other words, focus on what the variable represents, not how it is manipulated. Consider the following comment:

```
/* FOLLOWER VARIABLE: indicator variable that allows the Receiver and the
 * PeriodicTasks thread to communicate about whether a heartbeat has been
 * received within the follower's election timeout window.
 * Toggled to TRUE when a valid heartbeat is received.
 * Toggled to FALSE when the election timeout window is reset. */
private boolean receivedValidHeartbeat;
```

This documentation describes how the variable is modified by several pieces of code in the class. The comment will be both shorter and more useful if it describes what the variable represents rather than mirroring the code structure:

```
/* True means that a heartbeat has been received since the last time
 * the election timer was reset. Used for communication between the
 * Receiver and PeriodicTasks threads. */
private boolean receivedValidHeartbeat;
```

Given this documentation, it's easy to infer that the variable must be set to true when a heartbeat is received and false when the election timer is reset.

13.4   Higher-level comments enhance intuition

The second way in which comments can augment code is by providing intuition. These comments are written at a higher level than the code. They omit details and help the reader to understand the overall intent and structure of the code. This approach is commonly used for comments inside methods, and for interface comments. For example, consider the following code:

```
// If there is a LOADING readRpc using the same session
// as PKHash pointed to by assignPos, and the last PKHash
// in that readRPC is smaller than current assigning
// PKHash, then we put assigning PKHash into that readRPC.
int readActiveRpcId = RPC_ID_NOT_ASSIGNED;
for (int i = 0; i < NUM_READ_RPC; i++) {
```

```
    if (session == readRpc[i].session
            && readRpc[i].status == LOADING
            && readRpc[i].maxPos < assignPos
            && readRpc[i].numHashes < MAX_PKHASHES_PERRPC) {
        readActiveRpcId = i;
        break;
    }
}
```

The comment is too low-level and detailed. On the one hand, it partially repeats the code: "if there is a LOADING readRPC" just duplicates the test `readRpc[i].status == LOADING`. On the other hand, the comment doesn't explain the overall purpose of this code, or how it fits into the method that contains it. As a result, the comment doesn't help the reader to understand the code.

Here is a better comment:

```
// Try to append the current key hash onto an existing
// RPC to the desired server that hasn't been sent yet.
```

This comment doesn't contain any details; instead, it describes the code's overall function at a higher level. With this high-level information, a reader can explain almost everything that happens in the code: the loop must be iterating over all the existing remote procedure calls (RPCs); the `session` test is probably used to see if a particular RPC is destined for the right server; the `LOADING` test suggests that RPCs can have multiple states, and in some states it isn't safe to add more hashes; the `MAX_-PKHASHES_PERRPC` test suggests that there is a limit to how many hashes can be sent in a single RPC. The only thing not explained by the comment is the `maxPos` test. Furthermore, the new comment provides a basis for readers to judge the code: does it do everything that is needed to add the key hash to an existing RPC? The original comment didn't describe the overall intent of the code, so it's hard for a reader to decide whether the code is behaving correctly.

Higher-level comments are more difficult to write than lower-level comments because you must think about the code in a different way. Ask yourself: What is this code trying to do? What is the simplest thing you can say that explains everything in the code? What is the most important thing about this code?

Engineers tend to be very detail-oriented. We love details and are good at managing lots of them; this is essential for being a good engineer. But, great software designers can also step back from the details and think about a system at a higher level. This means deciding which aspects of the system are most important, and being able to ignore the low-level details and think about the system only in terms of its most fundamental characteristics. This is the essence of abstraction (finding a simple way to think about a complex entity), and it's also what you must do when writing higher-level comments. A good higher-level comment expresses one or a few simple ideas that provide a conceptual framework, such as "append to an existing RPC." Given the framework, it becomes easy to see how specific code statements relate to the overall goal.

Here is another code sample, which has a good higher-level comment:

```
if (numProcessedPKHashes < readRpc[i].numHashes) {
    // Some of the key hashes couldn't be looked up in
    // this request (either because they aren't stored
    // on the server, the server crashed, or there
    // wasn't enough space in the response message).
    // Mark the unprocessed hashes so they will get
    // reassigned to new RPCs.
    for (size_t p = removePos; p < insertPos; p++) {
        if (activeRpcId[p] == i) {
            if (numProcessedPKHashes > 0) {
                numProcessedPKHashes--;
            } else {
                if (p < assignPos)
                    assignPos = p;
                activeRpcId[p] = RPC_ID_NOT_ASSIGNED;
            }
        }
    }
}
```

This comment does two things. The second sentence provides an abstract description of what the code does. The first sentence is different: it explains (in high level terms) *why* the code is executed. Comments of the form "how we get here" are very useful for helping people to understand code. For example, when documenting a method, it can be very helpful to describe the conditions under which the method is most likely to be invoked (especially if the method is only invoked in unusual situations).

13.5   Interface documentation

One of the most important roles for comments is to define abstractions. Recall from Chapter 4 that an abstraction is a simplified view of an entity, which preserves essential information but omits details that can safely be ignored. Code isn't suitable for describing abstractions; it's too low level and it includes implementation details that shouldn't be visible in the abstraction. The only way to describe an abstraction is with comments. **If you want code that presents good abstractions, you must document those abstractions with comments.**

The first step in documenting abstractions is to separate *interface comments* from *implementation comments*. Interface comments provide information that someone needs to know in order to use a class or method; they define the abstraction. Implementation comments describe how a class or method works internally in order to implement the abstraction. It's important to separate these two kinds of comments, so that users of an interface are not exposed to implementation details. Furthermore, these two forms had better be different. **If interface comments must also describe the implementation, then the class or method is shallow.** This means that the act of writing comments can provide clues about the quality of a design; Chapter 15 will return to this idea.

The interface comment for a class provides a high-level description of the abstraction provided by the class, such as the following:

```
/**
 * This class implements a simple server-side interface to the HTTP
 * protocol: by using this class, an application can receive HTTP
 * requests, process them, and return responses. Each instance of
 * this class corresponds to a particular socket used to receive
 * requests. The current implementation is single-threaded and
 * processes one request at a time.
 */
public class Http {...}
```

This comment describes the overall capabilities of the class, without any implementation details or even the specifics of particular methods. It also describes what each instance of the class represents. Finally, the comments describe the limitations of the class (it does not support concurrent access from multiple threads), which may be important to developers contemplating whether to use it.

The interface comment for a method includes both higher-level information for abstraction and lower-level details for precision:

- The comment usually starts with a sentence or two describing the behavior of the method as perceived by callers; this is the higher-level abstraction.
- The comment must describe each argument and the return value (if any). These comments must be very precise, and must describe any constraints on argument values as well as dependencies between arguments.
- If the method has any side effects, these must be documented in the interface

comment. A side effect is any consequence of the method that affects the future behavior of the system but is not part of the result. For example, if the method adds a value to an internal data structure, which can be retrieved by future method calls, this is a side effect; writing to the file system is also a side effect.

• A method's interface comment must describe any exceptions that can emanate from the method.

• If there are any preconditions that must be satisfied before a method is invoked, these must be described (perhaps some other method must be invoked first; for a binary search method, the list being searched must be sorted). It is a good idea to minimize preconditions, but any that remain must be documented.

Here is the interface comment for a method that copies data out of a `Buffer` object:

```
/**
 * Copy a range of bytes from a buffer to an external location.
 *
 * \param offset
 *      Index within the buffer of the first byte to copy.
 * \param length
 *      Number of bytes to copy.
 * \param dest
 *      Where to copy the bytes: must have room for at least
 *      length bytes.
 *
 * \return
 *      The return value is the actual number of bytes copied,
 *      which may be less than length if the requested range of
 *      bytes extends past the end of the buffer. 0 is returned
 *      if there is no overlap between the requested range and
 *      the actual buffer.
 */
uint32_t
Buffer::copy(uint32_t offset, uint32_t length, void* dest)
...
```

The syntax of this comment (e.g., `\return`) follows the conventions of Doxygen, a program that extracts comments from C/C++ code and compiles them into Web pages. The goal of the comment is to provide all the information a developer needs in order to invoke the method, including how special cases are handled (note how this method follows the advice of Chapter 10 and defines out of existence any errors associated with the range specification). The developer should not need to read the body of the

111

method in order to invoke it, and the interface comment provides no information about how the method is implemented, such as how it scans its internal data structures to find the desired data.

For a more extended example, let's consider a class called `IndexLookup`, which is part of a distributed storage system. The storage system holds a collection of tables, each of which contains many objects. In addition, each table can have one or more indexes; each index provides efficient access to objects in the table based on a particular field of the object. For example, one index might be used to look up objects based on their name field, and another index might be used to look up objects based on their age field. With these indexes, applications can quickly extract all of the objects with a particular name, or all of those with an age in a given range.

The `IndexLookup` class provides a convenient interface for performing indexed lookups. Here is an example of how it might be used in an application:

```
query = new IndexLookup(table, index, key1, key2);
while (true) {
    object = query.getNext();
    if (object == NULL) {
        break;
    }
    ... process object ...
}
```

The application first constructs an object of type `IndexLookup`, providing arguments that select a table, an index, and a range within the index (for example, if the index is based on an age field, `key1` and `key2` might be specified as 21 and 65 to select all objects with ages between those values). Then the application calls the `getNext` method repeatedly. Each invocation returns one object that falls within the desired range; once all of the matching objects have been returned, `getNext` returns `NULL`. Because the storage system is distributed, the implementation of this class is somewhat complex. The objects in a table may be spread across multiple servers, and each index may also be distributed across a different set of servers; the code in the `IndexLookup` class must first communicate with all of the relevant index servers to collect information about the objects in the range, then it must communicate with the servers that actually store the objects in order to retrieve their values.

Now let's consider what information needs to be included in the interface comment for this class. For each piece of information given below, ask yourself whether a developer needs to know that information in order to use the class (my answers to the questions are at the end of the chapter, on page 120):

112

1. The format of messages that the IndexLookup class sends to the servers holding indexes and objects.
2. The comparison function used to determine whether a particular object falls in the desired range (is comparison done using integers, floating-point numbers, or strings?).
3. The data structure used to store indexes on servers.
4. Whether or not IndexLookup issues multiple requests to different servers concurrently.
5. The mechanism for handling server crashes.

Here is the original version of the interface comment for the IndexLookup class; the excerpt also includes a few lines from the class's definition, which are referred to in the comment:

```
/*
 * This class implements the client side framework for index range
 * lookups. It manages a single LookupIndexKeys RPC and multiple
 * IndexedRead RPCs. Client side just includes "IndexLookup.h" in
 * its header to use IndexLookup class. Several parameters can be set
 * in the config below:
 * - The number of concurrent indexedRead RPCs
 * - The max number of PKHashes a indexedRead RPC can hold at a time
 * - The size of the active PKHashes
 *
 * To use IndexLookup, the client creates an object of this class by
 * providing all necessary information. After construction of
 * IndexLookup, client can call getNext() function to move to next
 * available object. If getNext() returns NULL, it means we reached
 * the last object. Client can use getKey, getKeyLength, getValue,
 * and getValueLength to get object data of current object.
 */
class IndexLookup {
    ...
  private:
    /// Max number of concurrent indexedRead RPCs
    static const uint8_t NUM_READ_RPC = 10;
    /// Max number of PKHashes that can be sent in one
    /// indexedRead RPC
    static const uint32_t MAX_PKHASHES_PERRPC = 256;
    /// Max number of PKHashes that activeHashes can
    /// hold at once.
    static const size_t MAX_NUM_PK = (1 << LG_BUFFER_SIZE);
}
```

Before reading further, see if you can identify the problems with this comment. Here are the problems that I found:

- Most of the first paragraph concerns the implementation, not the interface. As one example, users don't need to know the names of the particular remote procedure calls used to communicate with the servers. The configuration parameters referred to in the second half of the first paragraph are all private variables that are relevant only to the maintainer of the class, not to its users. All of this implementation information should be omitted from the comment.
- The comment also includes several things that are obvious. For example, there's no need to tell users to include IndexLookup.h: anyone who writes C++ code will be able to guess that this is necessary. In addition, the text "by providing all necessary information" says nothing, so it can be omitted.

A shorter comment for this class is sufficient (and preferable):

```
/*
 * This class is used by client applications to make range queries
 * using indexes. Each instance represents a single range query.
 *
 * To start a range query, a client creates an instance of this
 * class. The client can then call getNext() to retrieve the objects
 * in the desired range. For each object returned by getNext(), the
 * caller can invoke getKey(), getKeyLength(), getValue(), and
 * getValueLength() to get information about that object.
 */
```

The last paragraph of this comment is not strictly necessary, since it mostly duplicates information in the comments for individual methods. However, it can be helpful to have examples in the class documentation that illustrate how its methods work together, particularly for deep classes with usage patterns that are nonobvious. Note that

Red Flag: Implementation Documentation Contaminates Interface

This red flag occurs when interface documentation, such as that for a method, describes implementation details that aren't needed in order to use the thing being documented.

the new comment does not mention NULL return values from getNext. This comment is not intended to document every detail of each method; it just provides high level information to help readers understand how the methods work together and when each method might be invoked. For details, readers can refer to the interface comments for individual methods. This comment also does not mention server crashes; that is because server crashes are invisible to users of this class (the system automatically recovers from them).

Now consider the following code, which shows the first version of the documentation for the isReady method in IndexLookup:

```
/**
 * Check if the next object is RESULT_READY. This function is
 * implemented in a DCFT module, each execution of isReady() tries
 * to make small progress, and getNext() invokes isReady() in a
 * while loop, until isReady() returns true.
 *
 * isReady() is implemented in a rule-based approach. We check
 * different rules by following a particular order, and perform
 * certain actions if some rule is satisfied.
 *
 * \return
 *      True means the next Object is available. Otherwise, return
 *      false.
 */
bool IndexLookup::isReady() { ... }
```

Once again, most of this documentation, such as the reference to DCFT and the entire second paragraph, concerns the implementation, so it doesn't belong here; this is one of the most common errors in interface comments. Some of the implementation documentation is useful, but it should go inside the method, where it will be clearly separated from interface documentation. In addition, the first sentence of the documentation is cryptic (what does RESULT_READY mean?) and some important information is missing. Finally, it isn't necessary to describe the implementation of getNext here. Here is a better version of the comment:

```
/*
 * Indicates whether an indexed read has made enough progress for
 * getNext to return immediately without blocking. In addition, this
 * method does most of the real work for indexed reads, so it must
 * be invoked (either directly, or indirectly by calling getNext) in
 * order for the indexed read to make progress.
 *
 * \return
```

115

```
*        True means that the next invocation of getNext will not block
*        (at least one object is available to return, or the end of the
*        lookup has been reached); false means getNext may block.
*/
```

This version of the comment provides more precise information about what "ready" means, and it provides the important information that this method must eventually be invoked if the indexed retrieval is to move forward.

13.6   Implementation comments: what and why, not how

Implementation comments are the comments that appear inside methods to help readers understand how they work internally. Most methods are so short and simple that they don't need any implementation comments: given the code and the interface comments, it's easy to figure out how a method works.

The main goal of implementation comments is to help readers understand *what* **the code is doing** (not how it does it). Once readers know what the code is trying to do, it's usually easy to understand how the code works. For short methods, the code only does one thing, which is already described in its interface comment, so no implementation comments are needed. Longer methods have several blocks of code that do different things as part of the method's overall task. Add a comment before each of the major blocks to provide a high-level (more abstract) description of what that block does. Here is an example:

```
// Phase 1: Scan active RPCs to see if any have completed.
```

For loops, it's helpful to have a comment before the loop that describes what happens in each iteration:

```
// Each iteration of the following loop extracts one request from
// the request message, increments the corresponding object, and
// appends a response to the response message.
```

Notice how this comment describes the loop at a more abstract and intuitive level; it doesn't go into any details about how a request is extracted from the request message or how the object is incremented. Loop comments are only needed for longer or more complex loops, where it may not be obvious what the loop is doing; many loops are short and simple enough that their behavior is already obvious.

In addition to describing *what* the code is doing, implementation comments are also useful to explain *why*. If there are tricky aspects to the code that won't be obvious from reading it, you should document them. For example, if a bug fix requires the

116

addition of code whose purpose isn't totally obvious, add a comment describing why the code is needed. For bug fixes where there is a well-written bug report describing the problem, the comment can refer to the issue in the bug tracking database rather than repeating all its details ("Fixes RAM-436, related to device driver crashes in Linux 2.4.x"). Developers can look in the bug database for more details (this is an example of avoiding duplication in comments, which will be discussed in Chapter 16).

For longer methods, it can be helpful to write comments for a few of the most important local variables. However, most local variables don't need documentation if they have good names. If all of the uses of a variable are visible within a few lines of each other, it's usually easy to understand the variable's purpose without a comment. In this case it's OK to let readers read the code to figure out the meaning of the variable. However, if the variable is used over a large span of code, then you should consider adding a comment to describe the variable. When documenting variables, focus on *what* the variable represents, not how it is manipulated in the code.

13.7 Cross-module design decisions

In a perfect world, every important design decision would be encapsulated within a single class. Unfortunately, real systems inevitably end up with design decisions that affect multiple classes. For example, the design of a network protocol will affect both the sender and the receiver, and these may be implemented in different places. Cross-module decisions are often complex and subtle, and they account for many bugs, so good documentation for them is crucial.

The biggest challenge with cross-module documentation is finding a place to put it where it will naturally be discovered by developers. Sometimes there is an obvious central place to put such documentation. For example, the RAMCloud storage system defines a Status value, which is returned by each request to indicate success or failure. Adding a Status for a new error condition requires modifying many different files (one file maps Status values to exceptions, another provides a human-readable message for each Status, and so on). Fortunately, there is one obvious place where developers will have to go when adding a new status value, which is the declaration of the Status enum. We took advantage of this by adding comments in that enum to identify all of the other places that must also be modified:

```
typedef enum Status {
    STATUS_OK                        = 0,
    STATUS_UNKNOWN_TABLET            = 1,
```

```
STATUS_WRONG_VERSION                = 2,
...
STATUS_INDEX_DOESNT_EXIST           = 29,
STATUS_INVALID_PARAMETER            = 30,
STATUS_MAX_VALUE                    = 30,

// Note: if you add a new status value you must make the
// following additional updates:
// (1) Modify STATUS_MAX_VALUE to have a value equal to the
//     largest defined status value, and make sure its definition
//     is the last one in the list. STATUS_MAX_VALUE is used
//     primarily for testing.
// (2) Add new entries in the tables "messages" and "symbols" in
//     Status.cc.
// (3) Add a new exception class to ClientException.h
// (4) Add a new "case" to ClientException::throwException to map
//     from the status value to a status-specific ClientException
//     subclass.
// (5) In the Java bindings, add a static class for the exception
//     to ClientException.java
// (6) Add a case for the status of the exception to throw the
//     exception in ClientException.java
// (7) Add the exception to the Status enum in Status.java, making
//     sure the status is in the correct position corresponding to
//     its status code.
}
```

New status values will be added at the end of the existing list, so the comments are also placed at the end, where they are most likely to be seen.

Unfortunately, in many cases there is not an obvious central place to put cross-module documentation. One example from the RAMCloud storage system was the code for dealing with zombie servers, which are servers that the system believes have crashed, but in fact are still running. Neutralizing zombie servers required code in several different modules, and these pieces of code all depend on each other. None of the pieces of code is an obvious central place to put documentation. One possibility is to duplicate parts of the documentation in each location that depends on it. However, this is awkward, and it is difficult to keep such documentation up to date as the system evolves. Alternatively, the documentation can be located in one of the places where it is needed, but in this case it's unlikely that developers will see the documentation or know where to look for it.

I have recently been experimenting with an approach where cross-module issues are documented in a central file called designNotes. The file is divided up into clearly labeled sections, one for each major topic. For example, here is an excerpt from the file:

```
...
Zombies
-------
A zombie is a server that is considered dead by the rest of the
cluster; any data stored on the server has been recovered and will
be managed by other servers. However, if a zombie is not actually
dead (e.g., it was just disconnected from the other servers for a
while) two forms of inconsistency can arise:
* A zombie server must not serve read requests once replacement
  servers have taken over; otherwise it may return stale data that
  does not reflect writes accepted by the replacement servers.
* The zombie server must not accept write requests once replacement
  servers have begun replaying its log during recovery; if it does,
  these writes may be lost (the new values may not be stored on the
  replacement servers and thus will not be returned by reads).

RAMCloud uses two techniques to neutralize zombies. First,
...
```

Then, in any piece of code that relates to one of these issues there is a short comment referring to the designNotes file:

```
// See "Zombies" in designNotes.
```

With this approach, there is only a single copy of the documentation and it is relatively easy for developers to find it when they need it. However, this has the disadvantage that the documentation is not near any of the pieces of code that depend on it, so it may be difficult to keep up-to-date as the system evolves.

13.8 Conclusion

The goal of comments is to ensure that the structure and behavior of the system is obvious to readers, so they can quickly find the information they need and make modifications to the system with confidence that they will work. Some of this information can be represented in the code in a way that will already be obvious to readers, but there is a significant amount of information that can't easily be deduced from the code. Comments fill in this information.

When following the rule that comments should describe things that aren't obvious from the code, "obvious" is from the perspective of someone reading your code for the first time (not you). When writing comments, try to put yourself in the mindset of the reader and ask yourself what are the key things he or she will need to know. If your code is undergoing review and a reviewer tells you that something is not obvious, don't argue with them; if a reader thinks it's not obvious, then it's not obvious. Instead of arguing, try to understand what they found confusing and see if you can clarify that, either with better comments or better code.

13.9   Answers to questions on page 113

Does a developer need to know each of the following pieces of information in order to use the IndexLookup class?

1. *The format of messages that the IndexLookup class sends to the servers holding indexes and objects.* No: this is an implementation detail that should be hidden within the class.
2. *The comparison function used to determine whether a particular object falls in the desired range (is comparison done using integers, floating-point numbers, or strings?).* Yes: users of the class need to know this information.
3. *The data structure used to store indexes on servers.* No: this information should be encapsulated on the servers; not even the implementation of IndexLookup should need to know this.
4. *Whether or not IndexLookup issues multiple requests to different servers concurrently.* Possibly: if IndexLookup uses special techniques to improve performance, then the documentation should provide some high-level information about this, since users may care about performance.
5. *The mechanism for handling server crashes.* No: RAMCloud recovers automatically from server crashes, so crashes are not visible to application-level software; thus, there is no need to mention crashes in the interface documentation for IndexLookup. If crashes were reflected up to applications, then the interface documentation would need to describe how they manifest themselves (but not the details of how crash recovery works).

Chapter 14

Choosing Names

Selecting names for variables, methods, and other entities is one of the most underrated aspects of software design. Good names are a form of documentation: they make code easier to understand. They reduce the need for other documentation and make it easier to detect errors. Conversely, poor name choices increase the complexity of code and create ambiguities and misunderstandings that can result in bugs. Name choice is an example of the principle that complexity is incremental. Choosing a mediocre name for a particular variable, as opposed to the best possible name, probably won't have much impact on the overall complexity of a system. However, software systems have thousands of variables; choosing good names for all of these will have a significant impact on complexity and manageability.

14.1 Example: bad names cause bugs

Sometimes even a single poorly named variable can have severe consequences. The most challenging bug I ever fixed came about because of a poor name choice. In the late 1980's and early 1990's my graduate students and I created a distributed operating system called Sprite. At some point we noticed that files would occasionally lose data: one of the data blocks suddenly became all zeroes, even though the file had not been modified by a user. The problem didn't happen very often, so it was exceptionally difficult to track down. A few of the graduate students tried to find the bug, but they were unable to make progress and eventually gave up. However, I consider any unsolved bug to be an intolerable personal insult, so I decided to track it down.

It took six months, but I eventually found and fixed the bug. The problem was actually quite simple (as are most bugs, once you figure them out). The file system code used the variable name `block` for two different purposes. In some situations, `block` referred to a physical block number on disk; in other situations, `block` referred to a logical block number within a file. Unfortunately, at one point in the code there was a `block` variable containing a logical block number, but it was accidentally used in a context where a physical block number was needed; as a result, an unrelated block on disk got overwritten with zeroes.

While tracking down the bug, several people, including myself, read over the faulty code, but we never noticed the problem. When we saw the variable `block` used as a physical block number, we reflexively assumed that it really held a physical block number. It took a long process of instrumentation, which eventually showed that the corruption *must* be happening in a particular statement, before I was able to get past the mental block created by the name and check to see exactly where its value came from. If different variable names had been used for the different kinds of blocks, such as `fileBlock` and `diskBlock`, it's unlikely that the error would have happened; the programmer would have known that `fileBlock` couldn't be used in that situation.

Unfortunately, most developers don't spend much time thinking about names. They tend to use the first name that comes to mind, as long as it's reasonably close to matching the thing it names. For example, `block` is a pretty close match for both a physical block on disk and a logical block within a file; it's certainly not a horrible name. Even so, it resulted in a huge expenditure of time to track down a subtle bug. Thus, you shouldn't settle for names that are just "reasonably close". Take a bit of extra time to choose great names, which are precise, unambiguous, and intuitive. The extra attention will pay for itself quickly, and over time you'll learn to choose good names quickly.

14.2   Create an image

When choosing a name, the goal is to create an image in the mind of the reader about the nature of the thing being named. A good name conveys a lot of information about what the underlying entity is, and, just as important, what it is not. When considering a particular name, ask yourself: "If someone sees this name in isolation, without seeing its declaration, its documentation, or any code that uses the name, how closely will they be able to guess what the name refers to? Is there some other name that will paint a clearer picture?" Of course, there is a limit to how much information you can put in a single name; names become unwieldy if they contain more than two or three words. Thus, the challenge is to find just a few words that capture the most important aspects of the entity.

Names are a form of abstraction: they provide a simplified way of thinking about a more complex underlying entity. Like other forms of abstraction, the best names are those that focus attention on what is most important about the underlying entity while omitting details that are less important.

14.3 Names should be precise

Good names have two properties: precision and consistency. Let's start with precision. The most common problem with names is that they are too generic or vague; as a result, it's hard for readers to tell what the name refers to; the reader may assume that the name refers to something different from reality, as in the `block` bug above. Consider the following method declaration:

```
/**
 * Returns the total number of indexlets this object is managing.
 */
int IndexletManager::getCount() {...}
```

The term "count" is too generic: count of what? If someone sees an invocation of this method, they are unlikely to know what it does unless they read its documentation. A more precise name like `getActiveIndexlets` or `numIndexlets` would be better: with one of these names, readers will probably be able to guess what the method returns without having to look at its documentation.

Here are some other examples of names that aren't precise enough, taken from various student projects:

- A project building a GUI text editor used the names `x` and `y` to refer to the position of a character in the file. These names are too generic. They could mean many things; for example, they might also represent the coordinates (in pixels) of a character on the screen. Someone seeing the name `x` in isolation is

 Red Flag: Vague Name

If a variable or method name is broad enough to refer to many different things, then it doesn't convey much information to the developer and the underlying entity is more likely to be misused.

unlikely to think that it refers to the position of a character within a line of text. The code would be clearer if it used names such as `charIndex` and `lineIndex`, which reflect the specific abstractions that the code implements.

- Another editor project contained the following code:

```
// Blink state: true when cursor visible.
private boolean blinkStatus = true;
```

The name `blinkStatus` doesn't convey enough information. The word "status" is too vague for a boolean value: it gives no clue about what a true or false value means. The word "blink" is also vague, since it doesn't indicate what is blinking. The following alternative is better:

```
// Controls cursor blinking: true means the cursor is visible,
// false means the cursor is not displayed.
private boolean cursorVisible = true;
```

The name `cursorVisible` conveys more information; for example, it allows readers to guess what a true value means (as a general rule, names of boolean variables should always be predicates). The word "blink" is no longer in the name, so readers will have to consult the documentation if they want to know why the cursor isn't always visible; this information is less important.

- A project implementing a consensus protocol contained the following code:

```
// Value representing that the server has not voted (yet) for
// anyone for the current election term.
private static final String VOTED_FOR_SENTINEL_VALUE = "null";
```

The name for this value indicates that it's special but it doesn't say what the special meaning is. A more specific name such as `NOT_YET_VOTED` would be better.

- A variable named `result` was used in a method with no return value. This name has multiple problems. First, it creates the misleading impression that it will be the return value of the method. Second, it provides essentially no information about what it actually holds, except that it is some computed value. The name should provide information about what the result actually is, such as `mergedLine` or `totalChars`. In methods that do actually have return values, then using the name `result` is reasonable. This name is still a bit generic, but readers can look at the method documentation to see its meaning, and it's helpful to know that the value will eventually become the return value.

Like all rules, the rule about choosing precise names has a few exceptions. For example, it's fine to use generic names like `i` and `j` as loop iteration variables, as long

124

as the loops only span a few lines of code. If you can see the entire range of usage of a variable, then the meaning of the variable will probably be obvious from the code so you don't need a long name. For example, consider the following code:

```
for (i = 0; i < numLines; i++) {
    ...
}
```

It's clear from this code that i is being used to iterate over each of the lines in some entity. If the loop gets so long that you can't see it all at once, or if the meaning of the iteration variable is harder to figure out from the code, then a more descriptive name is in order.

It's also possible for a name to be too specific, such as in this declaration for a method that deletes a range of text:

```
void delete(Range selection) {...}
```

The argument name selection is too specific, since it suggests that the text being deleted is always selected in the user interface. However, this method can be invoked on any range of text, selected or not. Thus, the argument name should be more generic, such as range.

If you find it difficult to come up with a name for a particular variable that is precise, intuitive, and not too long, this is a red flag. It suggests that the variable may not have a clear definition or purpose. When this happens, consider alternative factorings. For example, perhaps you are trying to use a single variable to represent several things; if so, separating the representation into multiple variables may result in a simpler definition for each variable. The process of choosing good names can improve your design by identifying weaknesses.

Red Flag: Hard to Pick Name

If it's hard to find a simple name for a variable or method that creates a clear image of the underlying object, that's a hint that the underlying object may not have a clean design.

14.4   Use names consistently

The second important property of good names is consistency. In any program there are certain variables that are used over and over again. For example, a file system manipulates block numbers repeatedly. For each of these common usages, pick a name to use for that purpose, and use the same name everywhere. For example, a file system might always use `fileBlock` to hold the index of a block within a file. Consistent naming reduces cognitive load in much the same way as reusing a common class: once the reader has seen the name in one context, they can reuse their knowledge and instantly make assumptions when they see the name in a different context.

Consistency has three requirements: first, always use the common name for the given purpose; second, never use the common name for anything other than the given purpose; third, make sure that the purpose is narrow enough that all variables with the name have the same behavior. This third requirement was violated in the file system bug at the beginning of the chapter. The file system used `block` for variables with two different behaviors (file blocks and disk blocks); this led to a false assumption about the meaning of a variable, which in turn resulted in a bug.

Sometimes you will need multiple variables that refer to the same general sort of thing. For example, a method that copies file data will need two block numbers, one for the source and one for the destination. When this happens, use the common name for each variable but add a distinguishing prefix, such as `srcFileBlock` and `dstFileBlock`.

Loops are another area where consistent naming can help. If you use names such as `i` and `j` for loop variables, always use `i` in outermost loops and `j` for nested loops. This allows readers to make instant (safe) assumptions about what's happening in the code when they see a given name.

14.5   A different opinion: Go style guide

Not everyone shares my views about naming. Some of the developers of the Go language argue that names should be very short, often only a single character. In a presentation on name choice for Go, Andrew Gerrand states that "long names obscure what the code does."[1] He presents this code sample, which uses single-letter variable names:

---

[1] https://talks.golang.org/2014/names.slide#1

```
func RuneCount(b []byte) int {
    i, n := 0, 0
    for i < len(b) {
        if b[i] < RuneSelf {
            i++
        } else {
            _, size := DecodeRune(b[i:])
            i += size
        }
        n++
    }
    return n
}
```

and argues that it is more readable than the following version, which uses longer names:

```
func RuneCount(buffer []byte) int {
    index, count := 0, 0
    for index < len(buffer) {
        if buffer[index] < RuneSelf {
            index++
        } else {
            _, size := DecodeRune(buffer[index:])
            index += size
        }
        count++
    }
    return count
}
```

Personally, I don't find the second version any more difficult to read than the first. If anything, the name count gives a slightly better clue to the behavior of the variable than n. With the first version I ended up reading through the code trying to figure out what n means, whereas I didn't feel that need with the second version. But, if n is used consistently throughout the system to refer to counts (and nothing else), then the short name will probably be clear to other developers.

The Go culture encourages the use of the same short name for multiple different things: ch for character or channel, d for data, difference, or distance, and so on. To me, ambiguous names like these are likely to result in confusion and error, just as in the block example.

Overall, I would argue that readability must be determined by readers, not writers. If you write code with short variable names and the people who read it find it easy to

127

understand, then that's fine. If you start getting complaints that your code is cryptic, then you should consider using longer names (a Web search for "go language short names" will identify several such complaints). Similarly, if I start getting complaints that long variable names make my code harder to read, then I'll consider using shorter ones.

Gerrand makes one comment that I agree with: "The greater the distance between a name's declaration and its uses, the longer the name should be." The earlier discussion about using loop variables named i and j is an example of this rule.

14.6 Conclusion

Well chosen names help to make code more obvious; when someone encounters the variable for the first time, their first guess about its behavior, made without much thought, will be correct. Choosing good names is an example of the investment mind-set discussed in Chapter 3: if you take a little extra time up front to select good names, it will be easier for you to work on the code in the future. In addition, you will be less likely to introduce bugs. Developing a skill for naming is also an investment. When you first decide to stop settling for mediocre names, you may find it frustrating and time-consuming to come up with good names. However, as you get more experience you'll find that it becomes easier; eventually, you'll get to the point where it takes almost no extra time to choose good names, so you will get the benefits almost for free.

Chapter 15

Write The Comments First
(Use Comments As Part Of The Design Process)

Many developers put off writing documentation until the end of the development process, after coding and unit testing are complete. This is one of the surest ways to produce poor quality documentation. The best time to write comments is at the *beginning* of the process, as you write the code. Writing the comments first makes documentation part of the design process. Not only does this produce better documentation, but it also produces better designs and it makes the process of writing documentation more enjoyable.

15.1 Delayed comments are bad comments

Almost every developer I have ever met puts off writing comments. When asked why they don't write documentation earlier, they say that the code is still changing. If they write documentation early, they say, they'll have to rewrite it when the code changes; better to wait until the code stabilizes. However, I suspect that there is also another reason, which is that they view documentation as drudge work; thus, they put it off as long as possible.

Unfortunately, this approach has several negative consequences. First, delaying documentation often means that it never gets written at all. Once you start delaying, it's easy to delay a bit more; after all, the code will be even more stable in a few more weeks. By the time the code has inarguably stabilized, there is a lot of it, which means the task of writing documentation has become huge and even less attractive. There's never a convenient time to stop for a few days and fill in all of the missing comments, and it's easy to rationalize that the best thing for the project is to move on and fix bugs or write the next new feature. This will create even more undocumented code.

Even if you do have the self-discipline to go back and write the comments (and don't fool yourself: you probably don't), the comments won't be very good. By this time in the process, you have checked out mentally. In your mind, this piece of code is done; you are eager to move on to your next project. You know that writing comments is the right thing to do, but it's no fun. You just want to get through it as quickly as possible. Thus, you make a quick pass over the code, adding just enough comments to look respectable. By now, it's been a while since you designed the code, so your memories of the design process are becoming fuzzy. You look at the code as you are writing the comments, so the comments repeat the code. Even if you try to reconstruct the design ideas that aren't obvious from the code, there will be things you don't remember. Thus, the comments are missing some of the most important things they should describe.

15.2 Write the comments first

I use a different approach to writing comments, where I write the comments at the very beginning:
- For a new class, I start by writing the class interface comment.
- Next, I write interface comments and signatures for the most important public methods, but I leave the method bodies empty.
- I iterate a bit over these comments until the basic structure feels about right.
- At this point I write declarations and comments for the most important class instance variables in the class.
- Finally, I fill in the bodies of the methods, adding implementation comments as needed.
- While writing method bodies, I usually discover the need for additional methods and instance variables. For each new method I write the interface comment before the body of the method; for instance variables I fill in the comment at the same time that I write the variable declaration.

When the code is done, the comments are also done. There is never a backlog of unwritten comments.

The comments-first approach has three benefits. First, it produces better comments. If you write the comments as you are designing the class, the key design issues will be fresh in your mind, so it's easy to record them. It's better to write the interface comment for each method before its body, so you can focus on the method's abstraction and interface without being distracted by its implementation. During the coding and testing process you will notice and fix problems with the comments. As a result, the comments improve over the course of development.

15.3   Comments are a design tool

The second, and most important, benefit of writing the comments at the beginning is that it improves the system design. Comments provide the only way to fully capture abstractions, and good abstractions are fundamental to good system design. If you write comments describing the abstractions at the beginning, you can review and tune them before writing implementation code. To write a good comment, you must identify the essence of a variable or piece of code: what are the most important aspects of this thing? It's important to do this early in the design process; otherwise you are just hacking code.

Comments serve as a canary in the coal mine of complexity. If a method or variable requires a long comment, it is a red flag that you don't have a good abstraction. Remember from Chapter 4 that classes should be deep: the best classes have very simple interfaces yet implement powerful functions. The best way to judge the complexity of an interface is from the comments that describe it. If the interface comment for a method provides all the information needed to use the method and is also short and simple, that indicates that the method has a simple interface. Conversely, if there's no way to describe a method completely without a long and complicated comment, then the method has a complex interface. You can compare a method's interface comment with the implementation to get a sense of how deep the method is: if the interface comment must describe all the major features of the implementation, then the method

 Red Flag: Hard to Describe

The comment that describes a method or variable should be simple and yet complete. If you find it difficult to write such a comment, that's an indicator that there may be a problem with the design of the thing you are describing.

is shallow. The same idea applies to variables: if it takes a long comment to fully describe a variable, it's a red flag that suggests you may not have chosen the right variable decomposition. Overall, the act of writing comments allows you to evaluate your design decisions early, so you can discover and fix problems.

Of course, comments are only a good indicator of complexity if they are complete and clear. If you write a method interface comment that doesn't provide all the information needed to invoke the method, or one that is so cryptic that it's hard to understand, then that comment doesn't provide a good measure of the method's depth.

15.4 Early comments are fun comments

The third and final benefit of writing comments early is that it makes comment-writing more fun. For me, one of the most enjoyable parts of programming is the early design phase for a new class, where I'm fleshing out the abstractions and structure for the class. Most of my comments are written during this phase, and the comments are how I record and test the quality of my design decisions. I'm looking for the design that can be expressed completely and clearly in the fewest words. The simpler the comments, the better I feel about my design, so finding simple comments is a source of pride. If you are programming strategically, where your main goal is a great design rather than just writing code that works, then writing comments should be fun, since that's how you identify the best designs.

15.5 Are early comments expensive?

Now let's revisit the argument for delaying comments, which is that it avoids the cost of reworking the comments as the code evolves. A simple back-of-the-envelope calculation will show that this doesn't save much. First, estimate the total fraction of development time that you spend typing in code and comments together, including time to revise code and comments; it's unlikely that this will be more than about 10% of all development time. Even if half of your total code lines are comments, writing comments probably doesn't account for more than about 5% of your total development time. Delaying the comments until the end will save only a fraction of this, which isn't very much.

Writing the comments first will mean that the abstractions will be more stable before you start writing code. This will probably save time during coding. In contrast, if you write the code first, the abstractions will probably evolve as you code, which will require more code revisions than the comments-first approach. When you consider all of these factors, it's possible that it might be faster overall to write the comments first.

15.6 Conclusion

If you haven't ever tried writing the comments first, give it a try. Stick with it long enough to get used to it. Then think about how it affects the quality of your comments, the quality of your design, and your overall enjoyment of software development. After you have tried this for a while, let me know whether your experience matches mine, and why or why not.

Chapter 16

Modifying Existing Code

Chapter 1 described how software development is iterative and incremental. A large software system develops through a series of evolutionary stages, where each stage adds new capabilities and modifies existing modules. This means that a system's design is constantly evolving. It isn't possible to conceive the right design for a system at the outset; the design of a mature system is determined more by changes made during the system's evolution than by any initial conception. Previous chapters described how to squeeze out complexity during the initial design and implementation; this chapter discusses how to keep complexity from creeping in as the system evolves.

16.1 Stay strategic

Chapter 3 introduced the distinction between tactical programming and strategic programming: in tactical programming, the primary goal is to get something working quickly, even if that results in additional complexity; in strategic programming, the most important goal is to produce a great system design. The tactical approach very quickly leads to a messy system design. If you want to have a system that is easy to maintain and enhance, then "working" isn't a high enough standard; you have to prioritize design and think strategically. This idea also applies when you are modifying existing code.

Unfortunately, when developers go into existing code to make changes such as bug fixes or new features, they don't usually think strategically. A typical mindset is "what is the smallest possible change I can make that does what I need?" Sometimes developers justify this because they are not comfortable with the code being modified; they worry that larger changes carry a greater risk of introducing new bugs. However, this results in tactical programming. Each one of these minimal changes introduces a few special cases, dependencies, or other forms of complexity. As a result, the system design gets just a bit worse, and the problems accumulate with each step in the system's evolution.

If you want to maintain a clean design for a system, you must take a strategic approach when modifying existing code. **Ideally, when you have finished with each change, the system will have the structure it would have had if you had designed it from the start with that change in mind**. To achieve this goal, you must resist the temptation to make a quick fix. Instead, think about whether the current system design is still the best one, in light of the desired change. If not, refactor the system so that you end up with the best possible design. With this approach, the system design improves with every modification.

This is also an example of the investment mindset introduced on page 15: if you invest a little extra time to refactor and improve the system design, you'll end up with a cleaner system. This will speed up development, and you will recoup the effort that you invested in the refactoring. Even if your particular change doesn't require refactoring, you should still be on the lookout for design imperfections that you can fix while you're in the code. Whenever you modify any code, try to find a way to improve the system design at least a little bit in the process. **If you're not making the design better, you are probably making it worse.**

As discussed in Chapter 3, an investment mindset sometimes conflicts with the realities of commercial software development. If refactoring the system "the right way" would take three months but a quick and dirty fix would take only two hours, you may have to take the quick and dirty approach, particularly if you are working against a tight deadline. Or, if refactoring the system would create incompatibilities that affect many other people and teams, then the refactoring may not be practical.

Nonetheless, you should resist these compromises as much as possible. Ask yourself "Is this the best I can possibly do to create a clean system design, given my current constraints?" Perhaps there's an alternative approach that would be almost as clean as the 3-month refactoring but could be done in a couple of days? Or, if you can't afford to do a large refactoring now, get your boss to allocate time for you to come back to it after the current deadline. Every development organization should plan to spend a small fraction of its total effort on cleanup and refactoring; this work will pay for itself over the long run.

16.2 Maintaining comments: keep the comments near the code

When you change existing code, there's a good chance that the changes will invalidate some of the existing comments. It's easy to forget to update comments when you modify code, which results in comments that are no longer accurate. Inaccurate comments are frustrating to readers, and if there are very many of them, readers begin to distrust all of the comments. Fortunately, with a little discipline and a couple of guiding rules, it's possible to keep comments up-to-date without a huge effort. This section and the following ones put forth some specific techniques.

The best way to ensure that comments get updated is to position them close to the code they describe, so developers will see them when they change the code. The farther a comment is from its associated code, the less likely it is that it will be updated properly. For example, the best place for a method's interface comment is in the code file, right next to the body of the method. Any changes to the method will involve this code, so the developer is likely to see the interface comments and update them if needed.

An alternative for languages like C and C++ that have separate code and header files, is to place the interface comments next to the method's declaration in the .h file. However, this is a long way from the code; developers won't see those comments when modifying the method's body, and it takes additional work to open a different file and find the interface comments to update them. Some might argue that interface comments should go in header files so that users can learn how to use an abstraction without having to look at the code file. However, users should not need to read either code or header files; they should get their information from documentation compiled by tools such as Doxygen or Javadoc. In addition, many IDEs will extract and present documentation to users, such as by displaying a method's documentation when the method's name is typed. Given tools such as these, the documentation should be located in the place that is most convenient for developers working on the code.

When writing implementation comments, don't put all the comments for an entire method at the top of the method. Spread them out, pushing each comment down to the narrowest scope that includes all of the code referred to by the comment. For example, if a method has three major phases, don't write one comment at the top of the method that describes all of the phases in detail. Instead, write a separate comment for each phase and position that comment just above the first line of code in that phase. On the other hand, it can also be helpful to have a comment at the top of a method's implementation that describes the overall strategy, like this:

```
// We proceed in three phases:
// Phase 1: Find feasible candidates
// Phase 2: Assign each candidate a score
// Phase 3: Choose the best, and remove it
```

Additional details can be documented just above the code for each phase.

In general, the farther a comment is from the code it describes, the more abstract it should be (this reduces the likelihood that the comment will be invalidated by code changes).

16.3   Comments belong in the code, not the commit log

A common mistake when modifying code is to put detailed information about the change in the commit message for the source code repository, but then not to document it in the code. Although commit messages can be browsed in the future by scanning the repository's log, a developer who needs the information is unlikely to think of scanning the repository log. Even if they do scan the log, it will be tedious to find the right log message.

When writing a commit message, ask yourself whether developers will need to use that information in the future. If so, then document this information in the code. An example is a commit message describing a subtle problem that motivated a code change. If this isn't documented in the code, then a developer might come along later and undo the change without realizing that they have re-created a bug. If you want to include a copy of this information in the commit message as well, that's fine, but the most important thing is to get it in the code. This illustrates the principle of placing documentation in the place where developers are most likely to see it; the commit log is rarely that place.

16.4   Maintaining comments: avoid duplication

The second technique for keeping comments up to date is to avoid duplication. If documentation is duplicated, it is more difficult for developers to find and update all of the relevant copies. Instead, try to document each design decision exactly once. If there are multiple places in the code that are affected by a particular decision, don't repeat the documentation at each of these points. Instead, find the most obvious single place to put the documentation. For example, suppose there is tricky behavior related

138

to a variable, which affects several different places where the variable is used. You can document that behavior in the comment next to the variable's declaration. This is a natural place that developers are likely to check if they're having trouble understanding code that uses the variable.

If there is no "obvious" single place to put a particular piece of documentation where developers will find it, create a designNotes file as described in Section 13.7. Or, pick the best of the available places and put the documentation there. In addition, add short comments in the other places that refer to the central location: "See the comment in xyz for an explanation of the code below." If the reference becomes obsolete because the master comment was moved or deleted, this inconsistency will be self-evident because developers won't find the comment at the indicated place; they can use revision control history to find out what happened to the comment and then update the reference. In contrast, if the documentation is duplicated and some of the copies don't get updated, there will be no indication to developers that they are using stale information.

Don't redocument one module's design decisions in another module. For example, don't put comments before a method call that explain what happens in the called method. If readers want to know, they should look at the interface comments for the method. Good development tools will usually provide this information automatically, for example, by displaying the interface comments for a method if you select the method's name or hover the mouse over it. Try to make it easy for developers to find appropriate documentation, but don't do it by repeating the documentation.

If information is already documented someplace outside to your program, don't repeat the documentation inside the program; just reference the external documentation. For example, if you write a class that implements the HTTP protocol, there's no need for you to describe the HTTP protocol inside your code. There are already numerous sources for this documentation on the Web; just add a short comment to your code with a URL for one of these sources. Another example is features that are already documented in a user manual. Suppose you are writing a program that implements a collection of commands, with one method responsible for implementing each command. If there is a user manual that describes those commands, there's no need to duplicate this information in the code. Instead, include a short note like the following in the interface comment for each command method:

```
// Implements the Foo command; see the user manual for details.
```

It's important that readers can easily find all the documentation needed to understand your code, but that doesn't mean you have to write all of that documentation.

16.5   Maintaining comments: check the diffs

One good way to make sure documentation stays up to date is to take a few minutes before committing a change to your revision control system to scan over all the changes for that commit; make sure that each change is properly reflected in the documentation. These pre-commit scans will also detect several other problems, such as accidentally leaving debugging code in the system or failing to fix TODO items.

16.6   Higher-level comments are easier to maintain

One final thought on maintaining documentation: comments are easier to maintain if they are higher-level and more abstract than the code. These comments do not reflect the details of the code, so they will not be affected by minor code changes; only changes in overall behavior will affect these comments. Of course, as discussed in Chapter 13, some comments do need to be detailed and precise. But in general, the comments that are most useful (they don't simply repeat the code) are also easiest to maintain.

Chapter 17

Consistency

Consistency is a powerful tool for reducing the complexity of a system and making its behavior more obvious. If a system is consistent, it means that similar things are done in similar ways, and dissimilar things are done in different ways. Consistency creates cognitive leverage: once you have learned how something is done in one place, you can use that knowledge to immediately understand other places that use the same approach. If a system is not implemented in a consistent fashion, developers must learn about each situation separately. This will take more time.

Consistency reduces mistakes. If a system is not consistent, two situations may appear the same when in fact they are different. A developer may see a pattern that looks familiar and make incorrect assumptions based on previous encounters with that pattern. On the other hand, if the system is consistent, assumptions made based on familiar-looking situations will be safe. Consistency allows developers to work more quickly with fewer mistakes.

17.1 Examples of consistency

Consistency can be applied at many levels in a system; here are a few examples.

Names. Chapter 14 has already discussed the benefits of using names in a consistent way.

Coding style. It is common nowadays for development organizations to have style guides that restrict program structure beyond the rules enforced by compilers. Modern style guides address a range of issues, such as indentation, curly-brace placement, order of declarations, naming, commenting, and restrictions on language features con-

141

sidered dangerous. Style guidelines make code easier to read and can reduce some kinds of errors.

Interfaces. An interface with multiple implementations is another example of consistency. Once you understand one implementation of the interface, any other implementation becomes easier to understand because you already know the features it will have to provide.

Design patterns. Design patterns are generally-accepted solutions to certain common problems, such as the model-view-controller approach to user interface design. If you can use an existing design pattern to solve the problem, the implementation will proceed more quickly, it is more likely to work, and your code will be more obvious to readers. Design patterns are discussed in more detail in Section 19.5.

Invariants. An invariant is a property of a variable or structure that is always true. For example, a data structure storing lines of text might enforce an invariant that each line is terminated by a newline character. Invariants reduce the number of special cases that must be considered in code and make it easier to reason about the code's behavior.

17.2 Ensuring consistency

Consistency is hard to maintain, especially when many people work on a project over a long time. People in one group may not know about conventions established in another group. Newcomers don't know the rules, so they unintentionally violate the conventions and create new conventions that conflict with existing ones. Here are a few tips for establishing and maintaining consistency:

Document. Create a document that lists the most important overall conventions, such as coding style guidelines. Place the document in a spot where developers are likely to see it, such as a conspicuous place on the project Wiki. Encourage new people joining the group to read the document, and encourage existing people to review it every once in a while. Several style guides from various organizations have been published on the Web; consider starting with one of these.

For conventions that are more localized, such as invariants, find an appropriate spot in the code to document them. If you don't write the conventions down, it's unlikely that other people will follow them.

Enforce. Even with good documentation, it's hard for developers to remember all of the conventions. The best way to enforce conventions is to write a tool that checks

142

for violations, and make sure that code cannot be committed to the repository unless it passes the checker. Automated checkers work particularly well for low-level syntactic conventions.

One of my recent projects had problems with line termination characters. Some developers worked on Unix, where lines are terminated by newlines; others worked on Windows, where lines are normally terminated by a carriage-return followed by a newline. If a developer on one system made a small edit to a file previously edited on the other system, the editor would sometimes replace all of the line terminators with ones appropriate for that system. This gave the appearance that every line of the file had been modified, which made it hard to track the meaningful changes. We established a convention that files should contain newlines only, but it was hard to ensure that every tool used by every developer followed the convention. Every time a new developer joined the project, we would experience a rash of line termination problems while that developer adjusted to the convention.

We eventually solved this problem by writing a short script that was executed automatically before changes are committed to the source code repository. The script checks all of the files that have been modified and aborts the commit if any of them contain carriage returns. The script can also be run manually to repair damaged files by replacing carriage-return/newline sequences with newlines. This instantly eliminated the problems, and it also helped train new developers.

Code reviews provide another opportunity for enforcing conventions and for educating new developers about the conventions. The more nit-picky that code reviewers are, the more quickly everyone on the team will learn the conventions, and the cleaner the code will be.

When in Rome ... The most important convention of all is that every developer should follow the old adage "When in Rome, do as the Romans do." When working in a new file, look around to see how the existing code is structured. Are all public variables and methods declared before private ones? Are the methods in alphabetical order? Do variables use "camel case," as in `firstServerName`, or "snake case," as in `first_server_name`? When you see anything that looks like it might possibly be a convention, follow it. When making a design decision, ask yourself if it's likely that a similar decision was made elsewhere in the project; if so, find an existing example and use the same approach in your new code.

Don't change existing conventions. Resist the urge to "improve" on existing conventions. **Having a "better idea" is not a sufficient excuse to introduce inconsistencies.**

143

Your new idea may indeed be better, but the value of consistency over inconsistency is almost always greater than the value of one approach over another. Before introducing inconsistent behavior, ask yourself two questions. First, do you have significant new information justifying your approach that wasn't available when the old convention was established? Second, is the new approach so much better that it is worth taking the time to update all of the old uses? If your organization agrees that the answers to both questions are "yes," then go ahead and make the upgrade; when you are done, there should be no sign of the old convention. However, you still run the risk that other developers will not know about the new convention, so they may reintroduce the old approach in the future. Overall, reconsidering established conventions is rarely a good use of developer time.

17.3   Taking it too far

Consistency means not only that similar things should be done in similar ways, but that dissimilar things should be done in different ways. If you become overzealous about consistency and try to force dissimilar things into the same approach, such as by using the same variable name for things that are really different or using an existing design pattern for a task that doesn't fit the pattern, you'll create complexity and confusion. Consistency only provides benefits when developers have confidence that "if it looks like an x, it really is an x."

17.4   Conclusion

Consistency is another example of the investment mindset. It will take a bit of extra work to ensure consistency: work to decide on conventions, work to create automated checkers, work to look for similar situations to mimic in new code, and work in code reviews to educate the team. The return on this investment is that your code will be more obvious. Developers will be able to understand the code's behavior more quickly and accurately, and this will allow them to work faster, with fewer bugs.

Chapter 18

Code Should be Obvious

Obscurity is one of the two main causes of complexity described in Section 2.3. Obscurity occurs when important information about a system is not obvious to new developers. The solution to the obscurity problem is to write code in a way that makes it obvious; this chapter discusses some of the factors that make code more or less obvious.

If code is obvious, it means that someone can read the code quickly, without much thought, and their first guesses about the behavior or meaning of the code will be correct. If code is obvious, a reader doesn't need to spend much time or effort to gather all the information they need to work with the code. If code is not obvious, then a reader must expend a lot of time and energy to understand it. Not only does this reduce their efficiency, but it also increases the likelihood of misunderstanding and bugs. Obvious code needs fewer comments than nonobvious code.

"Obvious" is in the mind of the reader: it's easier to notice that someone else's code is nonobvious than to see problems with your own code. Thus, the best way to determine the obviousness of code is through code reviews. If someone reading your code says it's not obvious, then it's not obvious, no matter how clear it may seem to you. By trying to understand what made the code nonobvious, you will learn how to write better code in the future.

18.1   Things that make code more obvious

Two of the most important techniques for making code obvious have already been discussed in previous chapters. The first is choosing good names (Chapter 14). Precise and meaningful names clarify the behavior of the code and reduce the need for documentation. If a name is vague or ambiguous, then readers will have read through the code in order to deduce the meaning of the named entity; this is time-consuming and error-prone. The second technique is consistency (Chapter 17). If similar things are always done in similar ways, then readers can recognize patterns they have seen before and immediately draw (safe) conclusions without analyzing the code in detail.

Here are a few other general-purpose techniques for making code more obvious:

Judicious use of white space. The way code is formatted can impact how easy it is to understand. Consider the following parameter documentation, in which whitespace has been squeezed out:

```
/**
 * ...
 * @param numThreads The number of threads that this manager should
 * spin up in order to manage ongoing connections. The MessageManager
 * spins up at least one thread for every open connection, so this
 * should be at least equal to the number of connections you expect
 * to be open at once. This should be a multiple of that number if
 * you expect to send a lot of messages in a short amount of time.
 * @param handler Used as a callback in order to handle incoming
 * messages on this MessageManager's open connections. See
 * {@code MessageHandler} and {@code handleMessage} for details.
 */
```

It's hard to see where the documentation for one parameter ends and the next begins. It's not even obvious how many parameters there are, or what their names are. If a little whitespace is added, the structure suddenly becomes clear and the documentation is easier to scan:

```
/**
 * @param numThreads
 *         The number of threads that this manager should spin up in
 *         order to manage ongoing connections. The MessageManager spins
 *         up at least one thread for every open connection, so this
 *         should be at least equal to the number of connections you
 *         expect to be open at once. This should be a multiple of that
 *         number if you expect to send a lot of messages in a short
 *         amount of time.
 * @param handler
 *         Used as a callback in order to handle incoming messages on
 *         this MessageManager's open connections. See
 *         {@code MessageHandler} and {@code handleMessage} for details.
 */
```

146

Blank lines are also useful to separate major blocks of code within a method, such as in the following example:

```
void* Buffer::allocAux(size_t numBytes)
{
    // Round up the length to a multiple of 8 bytes, to ensure alignment.
    uint32_t numBytes32 = (downCast<uint32_t>(numBytes) + 7) & ~0x7;
    assert(numBytes32 != 0);

    // If there is enough memory at firstAvailable, use that.  Work down
    // from the top, because this memory is guaranteed to be aligned
    // (memory at the bottom may have been used for variable-size chunks).
    if (availableLength >= numBytes32) {
        availableLength -= numBytes32;
        return firstAvailable + availableLength;
    }

    // Next, see if there is extra space at the end of the last chunk.
    if (extraAppendBytes >= numBytes32) {
        extraAppendBytes -= numBytes32;
        return lastChunk->data + lastChunk->length + extraAppendBytes;
    }

    // Must create a new space allocation; allocate space within it.
    uint32_t allocatedLength;
    firstAvailable = getNewAllocation(numBytes32, &allocatedLength);
    availableLength = allocatedLength - numBytes32;
    return firstAvailable + availableLength;
}
```

This approach works particularly well if the first line after each blank line is a comment describing the next block of code: the blank lines make the comments more visible.

White space within a statement helps to clarify the structure of the statement. Compare the following two statements, one of which has whitespace and one of which doesn't:

```
for(int pass=1;pass>=0&&!empty;pass--) {

for (int pass = 1; pass >= 0 && !empty; pass--) {
```

Comments. Sometimes it isn't possible to avoid code that is nonobvious. When this happens, it's important to use comments to compensate by providing the missing information. To do this well, you must put yourself in the position of the reader and figure out what is likely to confuse them, and what information will clear up that confusion. The next section shows a few examples.

147

18.2   Things that make code less obvious

There are many things that can make code nonobvious; this section provides a few examples. Some of these, such as event-driven programming, are useful in some situations, so you may end up using them anyway. When this happens, extra documentation can help to minimize reader confusion.

Event-driven programming. In event-driven programming, an application responds to external occurrences, such as the arrival of a network packet or the press of a mouse button. One module is responsible for reporting incoming events. Other parts of the application register interest in certain events by asking the event module to invoke a given function or method when those events occur.

Event-driven programming makes it hard to follow the flow of control. The event handler functions are never invoked directly; they are invoked indirectly by the event module, typically using a function pointer or interface. Even if you find the point of invocation in the event module, it still isn't possible to tell which specific function will be invoked: this will depend on which handlers were registered at runtime. Because of this, it's hard to reason about event-driven code or convince yourself that it works.

To compensate for this obscurity, use the interface comment for each handler function to indicate when it is invoked, as in this example:

```
/**
 * This method is invoked in the dispatch thread by a transport if a
 * transport-level error prevents an RPC from completing.
 */
void
Transport::RpcNotifier::failed() {
    ...
}
```

Red Flag: Nonobvious Code

If the meaning and behavior of code cannot be understood with a quick reading, it is a red flag. Often this means that there is important information that is not immediately clear to someone reading the code.

Generic containers. Many languages provide generic classes for grouping two or more items into a single object, such as `Pair` in Java or `std::pair` in C++. These classes are tempting because they make it easy to pass around several objects with a single variable. One of the most common uses is to return multiple values from a method, as in this Java example:

```
return new Pair<Integer, Boolean>(currentTerm, false);
```

Unfortunately, generic containers result in nonobvious code because the grouped elements have generic names that obscure their meaning. In the example above, the caller must reference the two returned values with `result.getKey()` and `result.get-Value()`, which give no clue about the actual meaning of the values.

Thus, it's better not to use generic containers. If you need a container, define a new class or structure that is specialized for the particular use. You can then use meaningful names for the elements, and you can provide additional documentation in the declaration, which is not possible with the generic container.

This example illustrates a general rule: **software should be designed for ease of reading, not ease of writing.** Generic containers are expedient for the person writing the code, but they create confusion for all the readers that follow. It's better for the person writing the code to spend a few extra minutes to define a specific container structure, so that the resulting code is more obvious.

Different types for declaration and allocation. Consider the following Java example:

```
private List<Message> incomingMessageList;
...
incomingMessageList = new ArrayList<Message>();
```

The variable is declared as a `List`, but the actual value is an `ArrayList`. This code is legal, since `List` is a superclass of `ArrayList`, but it can mislead a reader who sees the declaration but not the actual allocation. The actual type may impact how the variable is used (`ArrayLists` have different performance and thread-safety properties than other subclasses of `List`), so it is better to match the declaration with the allocation.

Code that violates reader expectations. Consider the following code, which is the main program for a Java application

```
public static void main(String[] args) {
    ...
    new RaftClient(myAddress, serverAddresses);
}
```

Most applications exit when their main programs return, so readers are likely to assume

149

that will happen here. However, that is not the case. The constructor for RaftClient creates additional threads, which continue to operate even though the application's main thread finishes. This behavior should be documented in the interface comment for the RaftClient constructor, but the behavior is nonobvious enough that it's worth putting a short comment at the end of main as well. The comment should indicate that the application will continue executing in other threads. Code is most obvious if it conforms to the conventions that readers will be expecting; if it doesn't, then it's important to document the behavior so readers aren't confused.

18.3 Conclusion

Another way of thinking about obviousness is in terms of information. If code is nonobvious, that usually means there is important information about the code that the reader does not have: in the RaftClient example, the reader might not know that the RaftClient constructor created new threads; in the Pair example, the reader might not know that result.getKey() returns the number of the current term.

To make code obvious, you must ensure that readers always have the information they need to understand it. You can do this in three ways. The best way is to reduce the amount of information that is needed, using design techniques such as abstraction and eliminating special cases. Second, you can take advantage of information that readers have already acquired in other contexts (for example, by following conventions and conforming to expectations) so readers don't have to learn new information for your code. Third, you can present the important information to them in the code, using techniques such as good names and strategic comments.

Chapter 19

Software Trends

As a way of illustrating the principles discussed in this book, this chapter considers several trends and patterns that have become popular in software development over the last few decades. For each trend, I will describe how that trend relates to the principles in this book and use the principles to evaluate whether that trend provides leverage against software complexity.

19.1 Object-oriented programming and inheritance

Object-oriented programming is one of the most important new ideas in software development over the last 30–40 years. It introduced notions such as classes, inheritance, private methods, and instance variables. If used carefully, these mechanisms can help to produce better software designs. For example, private methods and variables can be used to ensure information hiding: no code outside a class can invoke private methods or access private variables, so there can't be any external dependencies on them.

One of the key elements of object-oriented programming is inheritance. Inheritance comes in two forms, which have different implications for software complexity. The first form of inheritance is interface inheritance, in which a parent class defines the signatures for one or more methods, but does not implement the methods. Each subclass must implement the signatures, but different subclasses can implement the same methods in different ways. For example, the interface might define methods for performing I/O; one subclass might implement the I/O operations for disk files, and another subclass might implement the same operations for network sockets.

Interface inheritance provides leverage against complexity by reusing the same interface for multiple purposes. It allows knowledge acquired in solving one problem (such as how to use an I/O interface to read and write disk files) to be used to solve other problems (such as communicating over a network socket). Another way of thinking about this is in terms of depth: the more different implementations there are of an interface, the deeper the interface becomes. In order for an interface to have many implementations, it must capture the essential features of all the underlying implementations while steering clear of the details that differ between the implementations; this notion is at the heart of abstraction.

The second form of inheritance is implementation inheritance. In this form, a parent class defines not only signatures for one or more methods, but also default implementations. Subclasses can choose to inherit the parent's implementation of a method or override it by defining a new method with the same signature. Without implementation inheritance, the same method implementation might need to be duplicated in several subclasses, which would create dependencies between those subclasses (modifications would need to be duplicated in all copies of the method). Thus, implementation inheritance reduces the amount of code that needs to be modified as the system evolves; in other words, it reduces the change amplification problem described in Chapter 2.

However, implementation inheritance creates dependencies between the parent class and each of its subclasses. Class instance variables in the parent class are often accessed by both the parent and child classes; this results in information leakage between the classes in the inheritance hierarchy and makes it hard to modify one class in the hierarchy without looking at the others. For example, a developer making changes to the parent class may need to examine all of the subclasses to ensure that the changes don't break anything. Similarly, if a subclass overrides a method in the parent class, the developer of the subclass may need to examine the implementation in the parent. In the worst case, programmers will need complete knowledge of the entire class hierarchy underneath the parent class in order to make changes to any of the classes. Class hierarchies that use implementation inheritance extensively tend to have high complexity.

Thus, implementation inheritance should be used with caution. Before using implementation inheritance, consider whether an approach based on *composition* can provide the same benefits. For instance, it may be possible to use small helper classes to implement the shared functionality. Rather than inheriting functions from a parent, the original classes can each build upon the features of the helper classes.

If there is no viable alternative to implementation inheritance, try to separate the state managed by the parent class from that managed by subclasses. One way to do this is for certain instance variables to be managed entirely by methods in the parent class, with subclasses using them only in a read-only fashion or through other methods in the parent class. This applies the notion of information hiding within the class hierarchy to reduce dependencies.

Although the mechanisms provided by object-oriented programming can assist in implementing clean designs, they do not, by themselves, guarantee good design. For example, if classes are shallow, or have complex interfaces, or permit external access to their internal state, then they will still result in high complexity.

19.2   Agile development

Agile development is an approach to software development that emerged in the late 1990's from a collection of ideas about how to make software development more lightweight, flexible, and incremental; it was formally defined during a meeting of practitioners in 2001. Agile development is mostly about the process of software development (organizing teams, managing schedules, the role of unit testing, interacting with customers, etc.) as opposed to software design. Nonetheless, it relates to some of the design principles in this book.

One of the most important elements of agile development is the notion that development should be incremental and iterative. In the agile approach, a software system is developed in a series of iterations, each of which adds and evaluates a few new features; each iteration includes design, test, and customer input. In general, this is similar to the incremental approach advocated here. As mentioned in Chapter 1, it isn't possible to visualize a complex system well enough at the outset of a project to determine the best design. The best way to end up with a good design is to develop a system in increments, where each increment adds a few new abstractions and refactors existing abstractions based on experience. This is similar to the agile development approach.

One of the risks of agile development is that it can lead to tactical programming. Agile development tends to focus developers on features, not abstractions, and it encourages developers to put off design decisions in order to produce working software as soon as possible. For example, some agile practitioners argue that you shouldn't implement general-purpose mechanisms right away; implement a minimal special-purpose mechanism to start with, and refactor into something more generic later, once you know that it's needed. Although these arguments make sense to a degree, they argue against an investment approach, and they encourage a more tactical style of programming. This can result in a rapid accumulation of complexity.

Developing incrementally is generally a good idea, but **the increments of development should be abstractions, not features**. It's fine to put off all thoughts about a particular abstraction until it's needed by a feature. Once you need the abstraction, invest the time to design it cleanly; follow the advice of Chapter 6 and make it somewhat general-purpose.

19.3   Unit tests

It used to be that developers rarely wrote tests. If tests were written at all, they were written by a separate QA team. However, one of the tenets of agile development is that testing should be tightly integrated with development, and programmers should write tests for their own code. This practice has now become widespread. Tests are typically divided into two kinds: unit tests and system tests. Unit tests are the ones most often written by developers. They are small and focused: each test usually validates a small section of code in a single method. Unit tests can be run in isolation, without setting up a production environment for the system. Unit tests are often run in conjunction with a test coverage tool to ensure that every line of code in the application is tested. Whenever developers write new code or modify existing code, they are responsible for updating the unit tests to maintain proper test coverage.

The second kind of test consists of system tests (sometimes called integration tests), which ensure that the different parts of an application all work together properly. They typically involve running the entire application in a production environment. System tests are more likely to be written by a separate QA or testing team.

Tests, particularly unit tests, play an important role in software design because they facilitate refactoring. Without a test suite, it's dangerous to make major structural changes to a system. There's no easy way to find bugs, so it's likely that bugs will go undetected until the new code is deployed, where they are much more expensive to find and fix. As a result, developers avoid refactoring in systems without good test suites; they try to minimize the number of code changes for each new feature or bug fix, which means that complexity accumulates and design mistakes don't get corrected.

With a good set of tests, developers can be more confident when refactoring because the test suite will find most bugs that are introduced. This encourages developers to make structural improvements to a system, which results in a better design. Unit tests are particularly valuable: they provide a higher degree of code coverage than system tests, so they are more likely to uncover any bugs.

For example, during the development of the Tcl scripting language, we decided to

154

improve performance by replacing Tcl's interpreter with a byte-code compiler. This was a huge change that affected almost every part of the core Tcl engine. Fortunately, Tcl had an excellent unit test suite, which we ran on the new byte-code engine. The existing tests were so effective in uncovering bugs in the new engine that only a single bug turned up after the alpha release of the byte-code compiler.

19.4   Test-driven development

Test-driven development is an approach to software development where programmers write unit tests before they write code. When creating a new class, the developer first writes unit tests for the class, based on its expected behavior. None of the tests pass, since there is no code for the class. Then the developer works through the tests one at a time, writing enough code for that test to pass. When all of the tests pass, the class is finished.

Although I am a strong advocate of unit testing, I am not a fan of test-driven development. **The problem with test-driven development is that it focuses attention on getting specific features working, rather than finding the best design.** This is tactical programming pure and simple, with all of its disadvantages. Test-driven development is too incremental: at any point in time, it's tempting to just hack in the next feature to make the next test pass. There's no obvious time to do design, so it's easy to end up with a mess.

As mentioned in Section 19.2, the units of development should be abstractions, not features. Once you discover the need for an abstraction, don't create the abstraction in pieces over time; design it all at once (or at least enough to provide a reasonably comprehensive set of core functions). This is more likely to produce a clean design whose pieces fit together well.

One place where it makes sense to write the tests first is when fixing bugs. Before fixing a bug, write a unit test that fails because of the bug. Then fix the bug and make sure that the unit test now passes. This is the best way to make sure you really have fixed the bug. If you fix the bug before writing the test, it's possible that the new unit test doesn't actually trigger the bug, in which case it won't tell you whether you really fixed the problem.

19.5   Design patterns

A design pattern is a commonly used approach for solving a particular kind of problem, such as an iterator or an observer. The notion of design patterns was popularized by the book *Design Patterns: Elements of Reusable Object-Oriented Software* by Gamma, Helm, Johnson, and Vlissides, and design patterns are now widely used in object-oriented software development.

Design patterns represent an alternative to design: rather than designing a new mechanism from scratch, just apply a well-known design pattern. For the most part, this is good: design patterns arose because they solve common problems, and because they are generally agreed to provide clean solutions. If a design pattern works well in a particular situation, it will probably be hard for you to come up with a different approach that is better.

The greatest risk with design patterns is over-application. Not every problem can be solved cleanly with an existing design pattern; don't try to force a problem into a design pattern when a custom approach will be cleaner. Using design patterns doesn't automatically improve a software system; it only does so if the design patterns fit. As with many ideas in software design, the notion that design patterns are good doesn't necessarily mean that more design patterns are better.

19.6   Getters and setters

In the Java programming community, *getter* and *setter* methods are a popular design pattern. A getter and a setter are associated with an instance variable for a class. They have names like `getFoo` and `setFoo`, where `Foo` is the name of the variable. The getter method returns the current value of the variable, and the setter method modifies the value.

Getters and setters aren't strictly necessary, since instance variables can be made public. The argument for getters and setters is that they allow additional functions to be performed while getting and setting, such as updating related values when a variable changes, notifying listeners of changes, or enforcing constraints on values. Even if these features aren't needed initially, they can be added later without changing the interface.

Although it may make sense to use getters and setters if you must expose instance variables, it's better not to expose instance variables in the first place. Exposed instance variables mean that part of the class's implementation is visible externally, which violates the idea of information hiding and increases the complexity of the class's interface. Getters and setters are shallow methods (typically only a single line), so they add clutter to the class's interface without providing much functionality. It's better to avoid getters and setters (or any exposure of implementation data) as much as possible.

One of the risks of establishing a design pattern is that developers assume the pattern is good and try to use it as much as possible. This has led to overusage of getters and setters in Java.

19.7 Conclusion

Whenever you encounter a proposal for a new software development paradigm, challenge it from the standpoint of complexity: does the proposal really help to minimize complexity in large software systems? Many proposals sound good on the surface, but if you look more deeply you will see that some of them make complexity worse, not better.

Chapter 20

Designing for Performance

Up until this point, the discussion of software design has focused on complexity; the goal has been to make software as simple and understandable as possible. But what if you are working on a system that needs to be fast? How should performance considerations affect the design process? This chapter discusses how to achieve high performance without sacrificing clean design. The most important idea is still simplicity: not only does simplicity improve a system's design, but it usually makes systems faster.

20.1 How to think about performance

The first question to address is "how much should you worry about performance during the normal development process?" If you try to optimize every statement for maximum speed, it will slow down development and create a lot of unnecessary complexity. Furthermore, many of the "optimizations" won't actually help performance. On the other hand, if you completely ignore performance issues, it's easy to end up with a large number of significant inefficiencies spread throughout the code; the resulting system can easily be 5–10x slower than it needs to be. In this "death by a thousand cuts" scenario it's hard to come back later and improve the performance, because there is no single improvement that will have much impact.

The best approach is something between these extremes, where you use basic knowledge of performance to choose design alternatives that are "naturally efficient" yet also clean and simple. The key is to develop an awareness of which operations are fundamentally expensive. Here are a few examples of operations that are relatively expensive today:

159

- Network communication: even within a datacenter, a round-trip message exchange can take 10–50 μs, which is tens of thousands of instruction times. Wide-area round-trips can take 10–100 ms.
- I/O to secondary storage: disk I/O operations typically take 5–10 ms, which is millions of instruction times. Flash storage takes 10–100 μs. New emerging nonvolatile memories may be as fast as 1 μs, but this is still around 2000 instruction times.
- Dynamic memory allocation (`malloc` in C, `new` in C++ or Java) typically involves significant overhead for allocation, freeing, and garbage collection.
- Cache misses: fetching data from DRAM into an on-chip processor cache takes a few hundred instruction times; in many programs, overall performance is determined as much by cache misses as by computational costs.

The best way to learn which things are expensive is to run micro-benchmarks (small programs that measure the cost of a single operation in isolation). In the RAMCloud project, we created a simple program that provides a framework for micro-benchmarks. It took a few days to create the framework, but the framework makes it possible to add new micro-benchmarks in five or ten minutes. This has allowed us to accumulate dozens of micro-benchmarks. We use these both to understand the performance of existing libraries used in RAMCloud, and also to measure the performance of new classes written for RAMCloud.

Once you have a general sense for what is expensive and what is cheap, you can use that information to choose cheap operations whenever possible. In many cases, a more efficient approach will be just as simple as a slower approach. For example, when storing a large collection of objects that will be looked up using a key value, you could use either a hash table or an ordered map. Both are commonly available in library packages, and both are simple and clean to use. However, hash tables can easily be 5–10x faster. Thus, you should always use a hash table unless you need the ordering properties provided by the map.

As another example, consider allocating an array of structures in a language such as C or C++. There are two ways you can do this. One way is for the array to hold pointers to structures, in which case you must first allocate space for the array, then allocate space for each individual structure. It is much more efficient to store the structures in the array itself, so you only allocate one large block for everything.

If the only way to improve efficiency is by adding complexity, then the choice is more difficult. If the more efficient design adds only a small amount of complexity, and if the complexity is hidden, so it doesn't affect any interfaces, then it may be worthwhile (but beware: complexity is incremental). If the faster design adds a lot of implementation complexity, or if it results in more complicated interfaces, then it may be better to start off with the simpler approach and optimize later if performance turns out to be a problem. However, if you have clear evidence that performance will be important in a particular situation, then you might as well implement the faster approach immediately.

In the RAMCloud project one of our overall goals was to provide the lowest possible latency for client machines accessing the storage system over a datacenter network. As a result, we decided to use special hardware for networking, which allowed RAMCloud to bypass the kernel and communicate directly with the network interface controller to send and receive packets. We made this decision even though it added complexity, because we knew from prior measurements that kernel-based networking would be too slow to meet our needs. In most of the rest of the RAMCloud system we were able to design for simplicity; getting this one big issue "right" made many other things easier.

In general, simpler code tends to run faster than complex code. If you have defined away special cases and exceptions, then no code is needed to check for those cases and the system runs faster. Deep classes are more efficient than shallow ones, because they get more work done for each method call. Shallow classes result in more layer crossings, and each layer crossing adds overhead.

20.2 Measure before modifying

But suppose that your system is still too slow, even though you have designed it as described above. It's tempting to rush off and start making performance tweaks, based on your intuitions about what is slow. Don't do this! Programmers' intuitions about performance are unreliable. This is true even for experienced developers. If you start making changes based on intuition, you'll waste time on things that don't actually improve performance, and you'll probably make the system more complicated in the process.

Before making any changes, measure the system's existing behavior. This serves two purposes. First, the measurements will identify the places where performance tuning will have the biggest impact. It isn't sufficient just to measure the top-level system performance. This may tell you that the system is too slow, but it won't tell you why. You'll need to measure deeper to identify in detail the factors that contribute to overall performance; the goal is to identify a small number of very specific places

161

where the system is currently spending a lot of time, and where you have ideas for improvement. The second purpose of the measurements is to provide a baseline, so that you can re-measure performance after making your changes to ensure that performance actually improved. If the changes didn't make a measurable difference in performance, then back them out (unless they made the system simpler). There's no point in retaining complexity unless it provides a significant speedup.

20.3   Design around the critical path

At this point, let's assume that you have carefully analyzed performance and have identified a piece of code that is slow enough to affect the overall system performance. The best way to improve its performance is with a "fundamental" change, such as introducing a cache, or using a different algorithmic approach (balanced tree vs. list, for instance). Our decision to bypass the kernel for network communication in RAM-Cloud is an example of a fundamental fix. If you can identify a fundamental fix, then you can implement it using the design techniques discussed in previous chapters.

Unfortunately, situations will sometimes arise where there isn't a fundamental fix. This brings us to the core issue for this chapter, which is how to redesign an existing piece of code so that it runs faster. This should be your last resort, and it shouldn't happen often, but there are cases where it can make a big difference. The key idea is to design the code around the critical path.

Start off by asking yourself what is the smallest amount of code that must be executed to carry out the desired task in the common case. Disregard any existing code structure. Imagine instead that you are writing a new method that implements just the critical path, which is the minimum amount of code that must be executed in the the most common case. The current code is probably cluttered with special cases; ignore them in this exercise. The current code might pass through several method calls on the critical path; imagine instead that you could put all the relevant code in a single method. The current code may also use a variety of variables and data structures; consider only the data needed for the critical path, and assume whatever data structure is most convenient for the critical path. For example, it may make sense to combine multiple variables into a single value. Assume that you could completely redesign the system in order to minimize the code that must be executed for the critical path. Let's call this code "the ideal."

The ideal code probably clashes with your existing class structure, and it may not be practical, but it provides a good target: this represents the simplest and fastest that the code can ever be. The next step is to look for a new design that comes as close as possible to the ideal while still having a clean structure. You can apply all of the design ideas from previous chapters of this book, but with the additional constraint of keeping the ideal code (mostly) intact. You may have to add a bit of extra code to the ideal in order to allow clean abstractions; for example, if the code involves a hash table lookup, it's OK to introduce an extra method call to a general-purpose hash table class. In my experience it's almost always possible to find a design that is clean and simple, yet comes very close to the ideal.

One of the most important things that happens in this process is to remove special cases from the critical path. When code is slow, it's often because it must handle a variety of situations, and the code gets structured to simplify the handling of all the different cases. Each special case adds a little bit of code to the critical path, in the form of extra conditional statements and/or method calls. Each of these additions makes the code a bit slower. When redesigning for performance, try to minimize the number of special cases you must check. Ideally, there will be a single if statement at the beginning, which detects all special cases with one test. In the normal case, only this one test will need to be made, after which the the critical path can be executed with no additional tests for special cases. If the initial test fails (which means a special case has occurred) the code can branch to a separate place off the critical path to handle it. Performance isn't as important for special cases, so you can structure the special-case code for simplicity rather than performance.

20.4 An example: RAMCloud Buffers

Let's consider an example, in which the Buffer class of the RAMCloud storage system was optimized to achieve a speedup of about 2x for the most common operations.

RAMCloud uses Buffer objects to manage variable-length arrays of memory, such as request and response messages for remote procedure calls. Buffers are designed to reduce overheads from memory copying and dynamic storage allocation. A Buffer stores what appears to be a linear array of bytes, but for efficiency it allows the underlying storage to be divided into multiple discontiguous chunks of memory, as shown in Figure 20.1. A Buffer is created by appending *chunks* of data. Each chunk is either *external* or *internal*. If a chunk is external, its storage is owned by the caller; the Buffer keeps a reference to this storage. External chunks are typically used for large chunks in order to avoid memory copies. If a chunk is internal, the Buffer owns the storage for the chunk; data supplied by the caller is copied into the Buffer's internal storage.

163

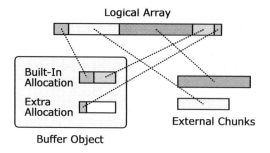

Logical Array

Built-In Allocation

Extra Allocation

Buffer Object

External Chunks

Figure 20.1: A Buffer object uses a collection of memory chunks to store what appears to be a linear array of bytes. Internal chunks are owned by the Buffer and freed when the Buffer is destroyed; external chunks are not owned by the Buffer.

Each Buffer contains a small built-in *allocation*, which is a block of memory available for storing internal chunks. If this space is exhausted, then the Buffer creates additional allocations, which must be freed when the Buffer is destroyed. Internal chunks are convenient for small chunks where the memory copying costs are negligible. Figure 20.1 shows a Buffer with 5 chunks: the first chunk is internal, the next two are external, and the final two chunks are internal.

The Buffer class itself represents a "fundamental fix," in that it eliminates expensive memory copies that would have been required without it. For example, when assembling a response message containing a short header and the contents of a large object in the RAMCloud storage system, RAMCloud uses a Buffer with two chunks. The first chunk is an internal one that contains the header; the second chunk is an external one that refers to the object contents in the RAMCloud storage system. The response can be collected in the Buffer without copying the large object.

Aside from the fundamental approach of allowing discontiguous chunks, we did not attempt to optimize the code of the Buffer class in the original implementation. Over time, however, we noticed Buffers being used in more and more situations; for example, at least four Buffers are created during the execution of each remote procedure call. Eventually, it became clear that speeding up the implementation of Buffer could have a noticeable impact on overall system performance. We decided to see if we could improve the performance of the Buffer class.

The most common operation for Buffer is to allocate space for a small amount of new data using an internal chunk. This happens, for example, when creating headers for request and response messages. We decided to use this operation as the critical path for optimization. In the simplest possible case, the space can be allocated by enlarging the last existing chunk in the Buffer. However, this is only possible if the last existing chunk is internal, and if there is enough space in its allocation to accommodate the new data. The ideal code would perform a single check to confirm that the simple approach is possible, then it would adjust the size of the existing chunk.

Figure 20.2 shows the original code for the critical path, which starts with the method `Buffer::alloc`. In the fastest possible case, `Buffer::alloc` calls `Buffer::allocateAppend`, which calls `Buffer::Allocation::allocateAppend`. From a performance standpoint, this code has two problems. The first problem is that numerous special cases are checked individually:

- `Buffer::allocateAppend` checks to see if the Buffer currently has any allocations.
- The code checks twice to see if the current allocation has enough room for the new data: once in `Buffer::Allocation::allocateAppend`, and again when its return value is tested by `Buffer::allocateAppend`.
- `Buffer::alloc` tests the return value from `Buffer::allocAppend` to confirm yet again that the allocation succeeded.

Furthermore, rather than trying to expand the last chunk directly, the code allocates new space without any consideration of the last chunk. Then `Buffer::alloc` checks to see if that space happens to be adjacent to the last chunk, in which case it merges the new space with the existing chunk. This results in additional checks. Overall, this code tests 6 distinct conditions in the critical path.

The second problem with the original code is that it has too many layers, all of which are shallow. This is both a performance problem and a design problem. The critical path makes two additional method calls in addition to the original invocation of `Buffer::alloc`. Each method call takes additional time, and the result of each call must be checked by its caller, which results in more special cases to consider. Chapter 7 discussed how abstractions should normally change as you pass from one layer to another, but all three of the methods in Figure 20.2 have identical signatures and they provide essentially the same abstraction; this is a red flag. `Buffer::allocateAppend` is nearly a pass-though method; its only contribution is to create a new allocation if needed. The extra layers make the code both slower and more complicated.

To fix these problems, we refactored the Buffer class so that its design is centered around the most performance-critical paths. We considered not just the allocation code

165

```
char* Buffer::alloc(int numBytes)
{
    char* data = allocateAppend(numBytes);
    Buffer::Chunk* lastChunk = this->chunksTail;
    if ((lastChunk != NULL && lastChunk->isInternal()) &&
            (data - lastChunk->length == lastChunk->data)) {
        // Fast path: grow the existing Chunk.
        lastChunk->length += numBytes;
        this->totalLength += numBytes;
    } else {
        // Creates a new Chunk out of the allocated data.
        append(data, numBytes);
    }
    return data;
}

// Allocates new space at the end of the Buffer; uses space at the end
// of the last current allocation, if possible; otherwise creates a
// new allocation. Returns a pointer to the new space.
char* Buffer::allocateAppend(int size) {
    void* data;
    if (this->allocations != NULL) {
        data = this->allocations->allocateAppend(size);
        if (data != NULL) {
            // Fast path
            return data;
        }
    }
    data = newAllocation(0, size)->allocateAppend(size);
    assert(data != NULL);
    return data;
}

// Tries to allocate space at the end of an existing allocation. Returns
// a pointer to the new space, or NULL if not enough room.
char* Buffer::Allocation::allocateAppend(int size) {
    if ((this->chunkTop - this->appendTop) < size)
        return NULL;
    char *retVal = &data[this->appendTop];
    this->appendTop += size;
    return retVal;
}
```

Figure 20.2: The original code for allocating new space at the end of a Buffer, using an internal chunk.

```
char* Buffer::alloc(int numBytes)
    if (this->extraAppendBytes >= numBytes) {
        // There is extra space at the end of the current
        // last chunk, so we can just allocate the new
        // region there.
        Buffer::Chunk* chunk = this->lastChunk;
        char* result = chunk->data + chunk->length;
        chunk->length += numBytes;
        this->extraAppendBytes -= numBytes;
        this->totalLength += numBytes;
        return result;
    }

    // We're going to have to create a new chunk.
    ...
}
```

Figure 20.3: The new code for allocating new space in an internal chunk of a Buffer.

above but several other commonly executed paths, such as retrieving the total number of bytes of data currently stored in a Buffer. For each of these critical paths, we tried to identify the smallest amount of code that must be executed in the common case. Then we designed the rest of the class around these critical paths. We also applied the design principles from this book to simplify the class in general. For example, we eliminated shallow layers and created deeper internal abstractions. The refactored class is 20% smaller than the original version (1476 lines of code, versus 1886 lines in the original).

Figure 20.3 shows the new critical path for allocating internal space in a Buffer. The new code is not only faster, but it is also easier to read, since it avoids shallow abstractions. The entire path is handled in a single method, and it uses a single test to rule out all of the special cases. The new code introduces a new instance variable, extraAppendBytes, in order to simplify the critical path. This variable keeps track of how much unused space is available immediately after the last chunk in the Buffer. If there is no space available, or if the last chunk in the Buffer isn't an internal chunk, or if the Buffer contains no chunks at all, then extraAppendBytes is zero. The code in Figure 20.3 represents the least possible amount of code to handle this common case.

Note: the update to totalLength could have been eliminated by recomputing the total Buffer length from the individual chunks whenever it is needed. However, this approach would be expensive for a large Buffer with many chunks, and fetching

167

the total Buffer length is another common operation. Thus, we chose to add a small amount of extra overhead to `alloc` in order to ensure that the Buffer length is always immediately available.

The new code is about twice as fast as the old code: the total time to append a 1-byte string to a Buffer using internal storage dropped from 8.8 ns to 4.75 ns. Many other Buffer operations also speeded up because of the revisions. For example, the time to construct a new Buffer, append a small chunk in internal storage, and destroy the Buffer dropped from 24 ns to 12 ns.

20.5 Conclusion

The most important overall lesson from this chapter is that clean design and high performance are compatible. The Buffer class rewrite improved its performance by a factor of 2 while simplifying its design and reducing code size by 20%. Complicated code tends to be slow because it does extraneous or redundant work. On the other hand, if you write clean, simple code, your system will probably be fast enough that you don't have to worry much about performance in the first place. In the few cases where you do need to optimize performance, the key is simplicity again: find the critical paths that are most important for performance and make them as simple as possible.

Chapter 21

Conclusion

This book is about one thing: complexity. Dealing with complexity is the most important challenge in software design. It is what makes systems hard to build and maintain, and it often makes them slow as well. Over the course of the book I have tried to describe the root causes that lead to complexity, such as dependencies and obscurity. I have discussed red flags that can help you identify unnecessary complexity, such as information leakage, unneeded error conditions, or names that are too generic. I have presented some general ideas you can use to create simpler software systems, such as striving for classes that are deep and generic, defining errors out of existence, and separating interface documentation from implementation documentation. And, finally, I have discussed the investment mindset needed to produce simple designs.

The downside of all these suggestions is that they create extra work in the early stages of a project. Furthermore, if you aren't used to thinking about design issues, then you will slow down even more while you learn good design techniques. If the only thing that matters to you is making your current code work as soon as possible, then thinking about design will seem like drudge work that is getting in the way of your real goal.

On the other hand, if good design is an important goal for you, then the ideas in this book should make programming more fun. Design is a fascinating puzzle: how can a particular problem be solved with the simplest possible structure? It's fun to explore different approaches, and it's a great feeling to discover a solution that is both simple and powerful. A clean, simple, and obvious design is a beautiful thing.

Furthermore, the investments you make in good design will pay off quickly. The modules you defined carefully at the beginning of a project will save you time later as you reuse them over and over. The clear documentation that you wrote six months ago will save you time when you return to the code to add a new feature. The time you spent honing your design skills will also pay for itself: as your skills and experience grow, you will find that you can produce good designs more and more quickly. Good design doesn't really take much longer than quick-and-dirty design, once you know how.

The reward for being a good designer is that you get to spend a larger fraction of your time in the design phase, which is fun. Poor designers spend most of their time chasing bugs in complicated and brittle code. If you improve your design skills, not only will you produce higher quality software more quickly, but the software development process will be more enjoyable.

Index

Summary of Design Principles

Here are the most important software design principles discussed in this book:

1. Complexity is incremental: you have to sweat the small stuff (see p. 11).

2. Working code isn't enough (see p. 14).

3. Make continual small investments to improve system design (see p. 15).

4. Modules should be deep (see p. 22)

5. Interfaces should be designed to make the most common usage as simple as possible (see p. 26).

6. It's more important for a module to have a simple interface than a simple implementation (see pp. 55, 71).

7. General-purpose modules are deeper (see p. 39).

8. Separate general-purpose and special-purpose code (see p. 62).

9. Different layers should have different abstractions (see p. 45).

10. Pull complexity downward (see p. 55).

11. Define errors (and special cases) out of existence (see p. 79).

12. Design it twice (see p. 91).

13. Comments should describe things that are not obvious from the code (see p. 101).

14. Software should be designed for ease of reading, not ease of writing (see p. 149).

15. The increments of software development should be abstractions, not features (see p. 154).

Summary of Red Flags

Here are a few of of the most important red flags discussed in this book. The presence of any of these symptoms in a system suggests that there is a problem with the system's design:

Shallow Module: the interface for a class or method isn't much simpler than its implementation (see pp. 25, 110).

Information Leakage: a design decision is reflected in multiple modules (see p. 31).

Temporal Decomposition: the code structure is based on the order in which operations are executed, not on information hiding (see p. 32).

Overexposure: An API forces callers to be aware of rarely used features in order to use commonly used features (see p. 36).

Pass-Through Method: a method does almost nothing except pass its arguments to another method with a similar signature (see p. 46).

Repetition: a nontrivial piece of code is repeated over and over (see p. 62).

Special-General Mixture: special-purpose code is not cleanly separated from general purpose code (see p. 65).

Conjoined Methods: two methods have so many dependencies that its hard to understand the implementation of one without understanding the implementation of the other (see p. 72).

Comment Repeats Code: all of the information in a comment is immediately obvious from the code next to the comment (see p. 104).

Implementation Documentation Contaminates Interface: an interface comment describes implementation details not needed by users of the thing being documented (see p. 114).

Vague Name: the name of a variable or method is so imprecise that it doesn't convey much useful information (see p. 123).

Hard to Pick Name: it is difficult to come up with a precise and intuitive name for an entity (see p. 125).

Hard to Describe: in order to be complete, the documentation for a variable or method must be long. (see p. 131).

Nonobvious Code: the behavior or meaning of a piece of code cannot be understood easily. (see p. 148).

Made in the USA
San Bernardino, CA
01 November 2018